Gateway to Science

from Yahoo! Ask Earl

Hiroshi Kazahaya

KINSEIDO

Kinseido Publishing Co.,Ltd.
3-21　Kanda Jimbo-cho, Chiyoda-ku,
Tokyo 101-0051, Japan
Copyright ©2006 by Hiroshi Kazahaya
All rights reserved. No part of this publication may be
reproduced, stored in a retrieval system, or transmitted,
in any form or by any means, electronic, mechanical,
photocopying, recording or otherwise, without the prior
permission of Kinseido Publishing Co., Ltd.

First published 2006 by Kinseido Publishing Co., Ltd.

Acknowledgments
Reproduced with permission of Yahoo! Inc. ©2004
by Yahoo! Inc. YAHOO! and the YAHOO! logo are
trademarks of Yahoo! Inc.

Design & illustration　Yukico Sugimoto

はしがき

　みなさんは自然の世界が持っている様々な現象に興味を持っているでしょうか。「クモの糸は何からできているの？」、「クモはどうして空を飛ぶの？」、「海水はなぜ塩辛いの？」、「オジギソウはなぜおじぎをするの？」、「インターネットはだれが発明したの？」などなど、世界は無限につづきそうな不思議でいっぱいです。

　実は筆者にも子供のころから不思議に思っていることがたくさんありますが、まだその答えを見出していないことばかりです。たとえば、最近は植物が持っている力に驚かされています。ある植物の枝を5センチくらいに切って土に挿しておくと、やがて根が出て半年くらいで大きく成長している。立派な花も咲きます。このような力は動物にはありませんね。「それは挿し木じゃないか。」で終わってしまったら実につまらないですが、ここから次々と疑問がわいてきます。根は、枝の土にさした側から発生してきますが、逆向きに挿し木をしたら、なぜ根が発生しないのか？植物はどのような仕組みで重力を感じ取っているのか？無重力の場所でも根が発生するのか？この段階で根に栄養を与えると、なぜ発根しにくくなるのか？

　このような疑問は子供じみているのかもしれません。しかし、そのような子供じみた疑問はとても重要な意義を持っているのだと考えます。たとえばさきほどの、オジギソウに関する疑問はダーウィンも持っていたようです。この植物のおじぎに関与する物質が発見されたのは、ごく最近のことらしいですね。発見者は日本人です。クモの糸の粘性はとても優れたもので、人間が合成しようとしても不可能に近いものらしいですね。

　具体的な話が少し長くなってしまいましたが、みなさんにもぜひ、子供じみた疑問をたくさん持っていただきたいと思います。そのことで毎日の生活はとても楽しいものになりますし、その疑問がやがて世界的な大発見につながるものになるかもしれません。この一冊がそのような意味でみなさんのお役に立てれば、これほど嬉しいことはありません。

さて、アメリカの子供たちも、様々な疑問を持っているのですね。かつてYAHOO! のサイトをなんとなく見ているうちに、このような疑問に大人が答えてあげるサイトがあることを偶然に発見しました。しばらく見ているうちに、その疑問が多岐にわたることに驚くとともに、日本の子供もおそらく同じような疑問を持っているのではないかと考えるにいたりました。あるいは、日本の高校生や大学生でもなかなか答えられない質問ではないのかとも思いました。

　質問も答えも英語ですが、これはかえって刺激的でいいですね。YAHOO! のサイトには、この種の質問がデータベースとして蓄積され、現在およそ1000種類くらいに及んでいますが、その中から日本人のみなさんにもぜひ考えていただけたらと思うものを100個ほど選びました。

　これらの質問や回答の内容は英語学習には最適の教材だと思います。質問に対する回答は、相手が(アメリカの)子供であることを十分に意識したものになっていますが、なかにはとても難しい専門用語が使われている場合もあります。そのような専門用語にはできるだけ(注)をつけましたが、なにしろ筆者は科学の分野に関しては、素人ですので思わぬ勘違いがあるかもしれません。そのような場合には、読者のみなさんがぜひご指摘をしてくださることを期待します。

　みなさんが、この本をきっかけに、自然の現象に対して大いなる疑問を持たれることを祈念いたします。なお、このサイトを出版することを快く承諾してくださったYAHOO! AMERICAの皆様と大変な仕事に最後までお付き合いくださった金星堂の方々にこの場を借りて御礼申し上げます。

2005年10月
風早　寛

Contents

Topic.1 Who invented the Internet?	P1
Topic.2 What is a spider's web made of ?	P2
Topic.3 Why is white chocolate white?	P3
Topic.4 How many cells in the human body?	P3
Topic.5 When were flutes first invented?	P4
Topic.6 How are CDs made?	P5
Topic.7 How does a cactus survive in the desert?	P6
Topic.8 How long do black bears live?	P7
Topic.9 Who was Ben Franklin?	P8
Topic.10 What do you know about malaria?	P9
Topic.11 What is the purpose of a skunk's stripe?	P9
Topic.12 Why do we sleep?	P10
Topic.13 How old is the oldest tree in the world?	P11
Topic.14 How fast do hummingbirds flap their wings?	P12
Topic.15 How many types of volcanoes are there and what are they?	P13
Topic.16 How do shells grow?	P14
Topic.17 Can you get milk from sheep?	P15
Topic.18 What is a vaccine?	P15
Topic.19 Where do cashews come from?	P16
Topic.20 How old is the Earth?	P17
Topic.21 How many teeth does an adult have?	P18
Topic.22 Do fish drink water?	P19
Topic.23 How old is the Great Barrier Reef?	P19
Topic.24 Who is the tallest person ever?	P20
Topic.25 Why are primary colors called primary?	P21
Topic.26 Why are cats afraid of water?	P22
Topic.27 What is genetic engineering?	P23
Topic.28 How did the planets get their names?	P25

Topic.29	Why is a banana a fruit? Where are the seeds?	P26
Topic.30	Who invented the telescope?	P27
Topic.31	How many species of pandas are there?	P28
Topic.32	How long would it take to get to Pluto?	P29
Topic.33	What do male mosquitoes eat?	P30
Topic.34	What is the most popular flavor of ice cream?	P31
Topic.35	Who invented electricity?	P31
Topic.36	Why does salt water exist?	P32
Topic.37	What percentage of people are lefties?	P34
Topic.38	Why do we sneeze?	P34
Topic.39	How long can a turtle stay underwater without coming up for air?	P35
Topic.40	Who invented the game of volleyball?	P36
Topic.41	Is there really trash up in space?	P37
Topic.42	Why are flamingoes pink?	P37
Topic.43	How many days does it take to get to Mars?	P38
Topic.44	What is narcolepsy?	P39
Topic.45	Are dolphins intelligent?	P40
Topic.46	Why does a satellite need a thermal blanket?	P41
Topic.47	Why do you have to brush your teeth?	P41
Topic.48	Why is some money on paper, and some in metal coins?	P42
Topic.49	Who invented the dictionary?	P43
Topic.50	How is cheese made?	P45
Topic.51	What is a desert?	P46
Topic.52	What is hypothermia?	P47
Topic.53	How fast does a cat run?	P48
Topic.54	What are the parts of the flower?	P49
Topic.55	Why are the waves in Australia and Hawaii so big?	P49
Topic.56	Who invented the compact disc?	P50

Contents 2

Topic.57	What is the smallest ocean?	P51
Topic.58	What do tigers eat?	P51
Topic.59	What are bones made of?	P52
Topic.60	What is friction?	P53
Topic.61	What is a lightning rod?	P53
Topic.62	How are coins made?	P54
Topic.63	What is censorship?	P55
Topic.64	How do clowns fit in their small car?	P56
Topic.65	What's the story behind potato chips?	P57
Topic.66	How long does it take for a dog to have puppies?	P58
Topic.67	What are windmills?	P59
Topic.68	Where does sand come from?	P60
Topic.69	How do you change between Celsius and Fahrenheit?	P61
Topic.70	What is a fossil?	P62
Topic.71	Why is Mars red?	P63
Topic.72	Do whales have teeth?	P64
Topic.73	What is a blizzard?	P65
Topic.74	How does your stomach work?	P65
Topic.75	How long can a person live without water?	P66
Topic.76	What is puberty?	P67
Topic.77	Why does your nose run when you cry?	P68
Topic.78	How was Jupiter formed?	P69
Topic.79	Why do roses have thorns?	P70
Topic.80	What is the smallest country?	P71
Topic.81	What is diabetes?	P72
Topic.82	Are dolphins mammals?	P73
Topic.83	Will sugar make water boil faster?	P74
Topic.84	How many satellites are there around the Earth?	P75

Topic.85　How far away are stars? What's the closest one?	P75
Topic.86　Who invented baseball?	P76
Topic.87　How does a battery work?	P77
Topic.88　How did the Earth form?	P78
Topic.89　Why is the sun yellow and not green?	P79
Topic.90　What is a fairy tale?	P79
Topic.91　What is celluloid exactly?	P80
Topic.92　How many animals give off their own light?	P81
Topic.93　Why does the moon shine?	P81
Topic.94　What did Jonas Salk invent?	P82
Topic.95　What was the largest tornado ever?	P83
Topic.96　How many different types of triangles are there?	P84
Topic.97　How come water has no taste or color?	P85
Topic.98　How do broken bones heal?	P86
Topic.99　Why do people yawn?	P86
Topic.100　How high can birds fly?	P87
Topic.101　What are amoebas?	P88
Topic.102　Are chimpanzees the smartest monkeys in the world?	P89
Topic.103　How many countries speak Spanish?	P90
Topic.104　How does yeast grow?	P92
Topic.105　Who invented the cassette tape?	P93
Topic.106　How are oceans formed?	P94
Topic.107　What is soil made of?	P95
Topic.108　Who invented popcorn?	P97
Topic.109　How do magnets work?	P97
Topic.110　How do cats land on their four legs when they fall?	P101
Topic.111　At what temperature does water boil?	P102

Gateway to Science

from Yahoo! Ask Earl

Who invented the Internet?

Topic.1

 There is no one inventor of the Internet. The Internet was created in the 1960s as a huge network linking big university and government computers. The science behind the Internet was invented during the Cold War, when the United States was in competition against Russia for weapons and technology. So the Internet is actually pretty old—around forty years. In fact, email has been around since 1972! But it wasn't until 1989 that Tim Berners-Lee, a scientist at the European Laboratory for Particle Physics in Geneva, proposed the World Wide Web.

|専門用語|
- □ World Wide Web　ワールド・ワイド・ウェブ (www)
- □ Tim Berners-Lee　ティム・バーナーズ・リー　□ Geneva　ジュネーブ

|注|
- □ There is no one inventor of the Internet.
  「たった一人の発明家がインターネットを発明したというものではない」
- □ in the 1960s　「1960年代に」
- □ huge network linking big university and government computers
  「大学や政府の大きなコンピュータをつなぐ巨大なネットワーク」
※ linkingは現在分詞で直前のnetworkを修飾している。
- □ Cold War
  「冷戦(=軍事行動には及ばないものの、互いに敵視しあっている国家間の対立状態)」
  (とはいえ、実際にはアメリカと旧ソ連との関係をさすことが多い)
- □ when the United States was in competition against Russia for weapons and technology
  「冷戦の時代には、アメリカはロシア(当時はソ連)に兵器や科学技術の分野で競争をしていた」
- □ So the Internet is actually pretty old—around forty years (old).
  「だからインターネットは実際にはかなり古くから存在したことになる。およそ40年くらい経過しているだろう」。「だから」というのは、「米ソの冷戦時代から存在していたのだから」ということ。
- □ email has been around　「emailは行き渡っている」
  cf. be around　「行き渡って、あちこちと」
- □ it wasn't until 1989 that …　「1989年になってはじめて…した」
  cf. It wasn't until 〜 that S V…　「〜になってはじめて…する」

> **参考**
>
> ティム・バーナーズ・リー
> (Timothy John Berners-Lee 1955年6月8日〜)は、WWWのハイパーテキストシステムを考案・開発した人物。WWWの概念の基礎となるEnquireを開発。URL、HTTP、HTMLの最初の設計は彼によるものである。
> World Wide Webプログラムは、1991年の夏には、インターネット上で広く稼働した。1994年に、マサチューセッツ工科大学のコンピュータサイエンス研究所に迎えられた。

What is a spider's web made of ?

Topic.2

Spiders have special organs underneath their abdomen called spinnerets. These organs produce the sticky material that's used for making webs, tying up prey, making cocoons, or spinning lines for floating. As you can see, it's a very useful material because it's very sticky but can also be quite strong. Spider webs are organic, meaning they come from the spider. In the same way that your mouth produces saliva to help you eat and digest food, spiders generate silk threads from their spinnerets.

専門用語
- □ spinneret 出糸突起 □ cocoon 繭、卵を包む袋繭
- □ saliva 唾液 □ silk thread 絹糸のような(クモの)糸

注
- □ tying up prey, making cocoons, or spinning lines for floating
 「獲物を縛ったり、卵を包む袋繭を作ったり、浮揚するための糸をつむいだりする」
- □ cocoon この語は通常は、「カイコの繭(まゆ)」をさすが、多くの種類のクモの中には、これと同類の保護用の袋を作る種類のクモもいる。
- □ lines for floating 「浮揚するための糸」。クモは移動手段として飛行することが知られている。特に小さめのクモは、風の強い日を選んで、突起から糸を出し、その糸に吹き付ける風の力を利用して空中に舞い上がる。セスナ機から捕虫網を出し上空の浮遊物を調査する実験において、多くの小さなクモが捕らえられた事実もある。
- □ As you can see
 「あなたにもわかってもらえると思うが」、「あなたもおわかりの通り」
- ※ このasは関係代名詞で、先行詞は後ろに書かれたit's a very useful material〜be quite strongの内容そのものである。関係代名詞のasはwhichと異なり、後ろの記述内容を先行詞にすることができる。

Why is white chocolate white?

White chocolate contains cocoa butter, milk solids, sugar, and vanilla; everything but "chocolate liquor," the thick dark paste that's produced by roasting and grinding the meat of the cocoa bean. This is the stuff that makes chocolate really chocolaty, and without it white chocolate is white and mild-flavored.

専門用語

□ chocolaty （形）チョコレートらしい (cf. Webster Online)

注

> **chocolate liquor**は、チョコレート・ココアの製造工場の用語で、カカオ豆から外皮を取り除いて磨砕して出来るペースト状のものをいう。これをチョコレートリカー（英：chocolate liquor）ということもある。チョコレートの主原料であるカカオ豆には52～58％のココアバターが含まれているが、ホワイトチョコレートは、この豆からチョコレート色の部分を除いた白色（淡黄色）のココアバターを主成分としている。カカオ豆の主成分であるココアバターを原料としているので、ホワイトチョコレートはチョコレート色をしていなくても立派なチョコレートだ。次のサイトはおもしろい。
> http://www.chocolate-cocoa.com/dictionary/dictionary1.htm

How many cells in the human body?

Every single living thing on Earth, from blue whales to barnacles, began as a single tiny cell. Cells are like the Lego blocks of life – there are many of them, and they each have a special role, or purpose. You have about seventy five trillion cells in your body. The different cells in your body – blood cells, bone cells, skin cells, and more – are constantly dying and regenerating. So it's safe to say that you're not the same person you were a year ago, or even a week ago!

[専門用語]
- blue whale　シロナガスクジラ(地球上の最大の生物。およそ35mで180トンにもなる)
- barnacle　フジツボ　　□ Lego　(商標)レゴ

[注]
- seventy five trillion cells　「75兆個の細胞」
- are constantly dying and regenerating
  「つねに死滅したり再生したりしている」
- It's safe to say that …　「…と言っても差しつかえない」

When were flutes first invented?

Topic.5

The flute is one of the oldest musical instruments − versions of it were used in Ancient Greece, during the second century BC! And if you've ever heard medieval music, you know that it's full of tootling flute sounds. In 1832 a famous flautist from the Bavarian Court Orchestra, Theobald Boehm, introduced the "ring key" system that is still used today. Flutes before that were very crude affairs: shaped like cones, with eight finger holes and only two keys. They were closer to recorders than flutes. But thanks to Mr. Boehm, you can now produce an amazing range of notes on your flute. Thanks, Theo!

[専門用語]
- tootle　(笛などが)ピーピーと鳴る　　□ flautist (英国) = flutist

[注]
- musical instrument　「楽器」
- versions of it　「(原型に対してその)異形、変形、改造されたもの」
- Bavarian Court Orchestra　「バイエルン宮廷オーケストラ」
- Theobald Boehm　「テオバルト・ベーム(ドイツ)」。色々な改良型のフルートを発表した。1847年にベーム・フルートと呼ばれる今日に至るフルートの原型を完成させた。
- affair　「(口語)もの、こと」

参考HP　http://cult.jp/traverso/hist.html

How are CDs made?

Music CDs have millions of tiny bumps and flat spaces that represent ones and zeros. The laser inside a CD player reads these ones and zeros and converts them into sound. To make a CD, a special machine uses a laser to imprint, or carve, those bumps and flat spaces onto thousands of discs at a time. The compact discs are then coated with aluminium so that the CD player's laser can read them, and then given a protective plastic coating.

専門用語

☐ bump　隆起、でこぼこ　☐ imprint（〜を）刻み込む

注

☐ represent ones and zeros　「1と0を表す」(コンピュータの世界では、計算は0と1から成る2進法で行う。)
☐ at a time　「一度に」
☐ so that the CD player's laser can read them
　「CDプレーヤーのレーザーが隆起の部分や平らな部分を読むことができるように」
※ so that S can …　「S が…できるように」
☐ and then (the compact discs are) given a protective plastic coating
　「それからコンパクトディスクはプラスチックコーティングで保護される」

なお、次のサイトを参考にするとよい。
http://www.ntv.co.jp/megaten/library/date/03/07/0720.html
エジソンが蓄音機を発明してからおよそ100年後の1982年、オランダのフィリップスという会社がコンパクトディスクという名の新しい商品を発表した。
　その方式は、まず音波というアナログの信号を44,100分の1秒ごとのパルス信号に変え、これを0と1の組み合わせからなるデジタル信号に置き換える。次に、その0と1の符号をディスク上に突起が「ある・ない」で記録する。
　再生する場合、突起の「ある・ない」は光で読み取る。レーザー光を当てると、突起がなければ発射口の方に反射し、突起があれば左右に散乱してしまう。この突起の「ある・ない」というデジタル信号をもとのアナログ信号に変えれば、音を再生することができるということがコンパクトディスクの原理だ。
　なお、DVDはCDによく似ている。DVDとCDは大きさ、厚さ共に、全く同じ。ではどこが違うか？原子力間顕微鏡でDVDとCDの表面を拡大すると、CDに比べDVDの方がデコボコが細かくついていた。CDはフロッピーディスク450枚分の情報量、一方DVDは3200枚分だ。

How does a cactus survive in the desert?

Topic.7

　Cacti (that's the plural of "cactus"!) are succulents. These plants can store lots of water in their leaves, stems, or roots so they can survive droughts and desert conditions. Even deserts get a little rain during the year, and when it rains, cacti suck up as much water as possible. Then they can live off that water during the dry season. The spines on a cactus also help it survive. Sharp spines make it harder for animals to eat the cactus. Spines also slow down blowing wind, which makes less water evaporate on and around the cactus. While cacti are found in sandy deserts, they're also found in semi-desert areas, dry grasslands, sub-alpine mountains, and even tropical jungles.

専門用語
- □ succulent　多肉植物　□ spine　とげ　□ grasslands　大草原
- □ sub-alpine　アルプス山麓地方の

注
- □ store lots of water　「多量の水分をたくわえる」
- □ so they can survive droughts and desert conditions
  「干ばつや砂漠の状況を切り抜けて生きることができるように」
- ※ so S can … = so that S can …　「S が…できるように」
- □ suck up as much water as possible　「できるだけたくさんの水分を吸い上げる」
- □ live off that water ＝ live on that water「(吸い上げた)その水で生きる」
- □ dry season　「乾季」(反対は雨季)
- □ help it survive　「サボテンが生き残るのに役立つ」
- ※ help O ＋(動詞の)原形 →「〜が…するのを助ける、役立つ」
- □ Sharp spines make it harder for animals to eat the cactus.
  「サボテンの鋭いとげは、動物がサボテンを食べることをより困難にする」
- □ blowing wind　「ふいている風」
- □ makes less water evaporate　「水分の蒸発を減らす」
- □ on and around the cactus　「サボテンの表面やまわりの」
- □ semi-desert　「半砂漠(地帯)」。草木がまばらにしか見られない砂漠とステップの中間の乾燥地帯。
- ※ semi- は「半…、部分的…」を表す。

How long do black bears live?

　How long a black bear lives depends on where it lives and how lucky it is. They can live up to 30 years, but only if they're protected. Most bears in the wild live to be about 10 years old. Very few adult bears die of natural causes – most are killed by people, either shot or hit by cars. Take a look at these pictures of black bears, and you'll see that they're not always black. Sometimes, they have a white patch of fur on their chests, or their fur is cinnamon brown.

専門用語
□ black bear　クロクマ

注

> How long a black bear lives depends on where it lives and how lucky it is.
> 　　　　　　S　　　　　　　　　V　　　　　　　　　　O
> 名詞節(＝疑問詞＋ＳＶ…)は主語にも目的語にもなれるから、depend on ～ (～次第だ)を述語動詞と考えれば、SVOの第３文型の英文である。
> 「クロクマがどれくらい長く生きるものなのかは、それがどこに住んでいるのかと、どれくらい幸運であるか次第である」

□ up to 30 years　「最高で30年まで」
※ up to ～　「～まで」
□ live to be ～　「～まで生きる」
□ a white patch of fur on their chests
　「胸のところに白色のまだらが(ある)」。日本のツキノワグマもクロクマの一種なので、ここではそのことを言っているのであろう。

memo

Who was Ben Franklin?

Benjamin Franklin was one of America's founding fathers. He lived from 1706 to 1790. He started life as a printer, and he published a newspaper and wrote a very popular book of advice called *Poor Richard's Almanack*. After Franklin retired from printing, he experimented with science and inventions. He learned about electricity and created the lightning rod. He also invented bifocal glasses and a practical wood stove. When the American colonies began to fight for independence, Franklin got involved too. He represented the colonies in Britain and negotiated a treaty with France. Franklin helped write both the Declaration of Independence and the U.S. Constitution. He did so much for the country that his face is now on the $100 bill!

専門用語
- bifocal glasses　二焦点(遠近両用)メガネ

注
- founding father　「建国の父」
- ※ found - founded - founded
- book of advice called *Poor Richard's Almanack*
  処世訓、格言を記した「貧しいリチャードの暦」
- printing　「印刷業」
- experiment with ～　「～の実験をする」
- lightning rod　「避雷針」
- American colonies
  「(イギリスがアメリカに最初に建設した)東部13州の植民地」
- get involved　「関わり合う」
- the colonies in Britain　「イギリスのアメリカ植民地」
- helped write ～
  = helped to write ～　「～を書くことに役立つ」
- the Declaration of Independence　「(米国の)独立宣言(1776年7月4日)」
- constitution　「憲法」

What do you know about malaria?

It's something to be careful of if you visit the tropics. Malaria is a life-threatening disease caused by a parasite, and it's spread by mosquitoes in the tropical parts of the world. When a female mosquito bites someone, the parasite gets into the person's blood. The disease causes fever, headache, and flu-like symptoms, and if it's not treated, it can kill. 90% of deaths from malaria are in Africa, where the malaria parasites have become resistant to some drugs used to treat the disease. So if you're going on safari in the future, avoid those mosquitoes, OK?

[専門用語]
☐ life-threatening　生命を脅かす

[注]
☐ something to be careful of　「注意すべきもの」
☐ flu-like　「インフルエンザに似た」
※ 接尾辞 -like は、名詞に付けて、「〜のような、〜に似た」という意味を持つ。
☐ have become resistant to some drugs　「薬に抵抗力を持つようになった」
☐ some drugs used to treat the disease　「マラリアを治療するために使われる薬」

What is the purpose of a skunk's stripe?

The bold white stripes running down the back of a skunk is a sign to other animals. What does that sign say? WATCH OUT OR I WILL STINK YOU UP BIG TIME! Well, maybe not those words exactly, but many other kinds of animals have bright colors to warn predators that they are dangerous. South American tree frogs, for instance, have brilliant red and green skins, and those skins are poisonous! And if a skunk sprays you, don't bother washing your clothes – just throw them away!

専門用語
- stink up ～　(場所など)を臭くする
- big time　全くひどく、完全に　□ predator　捕食者

注
- running down the back of a skunk
「スカンクの背中を流れて下っている」。直前のstripesを修飾している。
- sign to other animals　「他の動物への合図」
- watch out　「気をつける」
- maybe not those words exactly　「たぶん、その言葉通りではないだろうが」
- warn predators that S V…　「捕食者に…だということを警告する」
※ 動詞warn はこのような形の第4文型をとることができる点に注意。
- tree frog　「アオガエル」
- don't bother washing your clothes　「わざわざ衣服を洗濯する必要はない」
※ botherは、通例否定文で「わざわざ〔…〕する〔to do, (about) doing〕。ただ、to do の方が普通。

Why do we sleep?

Topic.12

During sleep, your muscles relax, your breathing slows, and your heart rate decreases. Sleep is your body's way of resting after a day of thinking and moving. If you miss a night's sleep, your reactions will slow and you'll feel pretty cranky. Your brain doesn't turn off completely when you sleep, which is why you dream. Scientists aren't sure if dreams have a purpose, or they're just the mind's way of blowing off steam. Either way, they're pretty weird and cool. Try writing your dreams down after you have them, so you won't forget!

専門用語
- cranky　気難しい、不安定な

注
- heart rate　「心拍数」
- after a day of thinking and moving　「一日考えたり動いたりした後で」
- miss a night's sleep　「一晩の眠りを欠かす」
- turn off　「(電気・ガスなどが)止まる」

Why do we sleep?

注
- □ not…completely 「完全に…するわけではない」(部分否定)
- □ ,which is why you dream 「そういう訳で夢を見るのだ」
- ※ ,whichの先行詞は前文の内容。
- □ Scientists aren't sure if S V… 「科学者は…かどうかについて確信が持てない」
- □ blow off steam 「ストレスを解消する」
- □ either way 「どちらにしても」。副詞的に用いることも多い。
- □ weird and cool 「奇妙なものであり、またすごいものでもある」
- □ Try writing your dreams down 「夢を書き留めてごらんよ」
- ※ try …ing 「ためしに…してみる」
- ※ write down ～ 「～を書き留める」

Topic.12

How old is the oldest tree in the world?

There is a bristlecone pine tree in California's White Mountains (in the Sierra Nevada mountain range) that's not just the oldest tree on Earth, but the oldest living thing on Earth! Called the Methuselah Tree, it was a seedling before the time of the Egyptian Pyramids. Biologists estimate that this tree is over 4,600 years old. It is named after a Biblical character who was said to be a thousand years old. Bristlecone pine trees can survive so long for a number of reasons: they grow high in the mountains so they have no competition, they prefer to stay small and grow close to the ground, and they are excellent at holding on to water.

専門用語
- □ bristlecone pine tree　ブリスルコーン・マツ
- □ the Sierra Nevada mountain range
  「シエラネバダ山脈(米国カリフォルニア州東部をを南北に走る山脈)」
- ※ mountain range 「山脈」
- □ Methuselah 「(聖書)メトセラ(旧約聖書の族長。969歳まで生きたとされる)」
- □ seedling 「実生(みしょう)の木」
- □ that's not just the oldest tree on Earth, but the oldest living thing on Earth!
  「地球上でもっとも古い木だというだけでなく、もっとも古い生物なのだ」
- ※ not just ～ but (also) … = not just ～ but (also) … 「～だけでなく…も」

注

- □ Called the Methuselah Tree 「メトセラの木と呼ばれて」
- ※ 分詞構文になっている。
- □ the time of the Egyptian Pyramids 「エジプトのピラミッドの時代」
- □ estimate that S V … 「…だと推定する」
- □ be named after 〜 「〜にちなんで名づけられる」
- □ Biblical character 「聖書の登場人物」
- □ for a number of reasons 「いくつもの理由で」
- □ grow high in the mountains 「山々の高いところで成長する」。
- ※ highは副詞。
- □ stay small 「小さいままでいる、大きくならない」
- ※ stay + 形容詞 「…のままでいる」
- □ close to the ground 「地面近くで」
- □ hold on to 〜 「〜を離さない、〜を手放さない」
- □ be excellent at 〜 「〜に優れている」

How fast do hummingbirds flap their wings?

Topic.14

Most hummingbirds flap their wings fifty-five times per second! They're also very fast, and can fly up to twenty-five miles per hour. All hummingbirds defend their food, even after they've stuffed themselves. A hummingbird will make an angry buzzing sound with their wings if they feel like someone is trying to steal their dinner. Their wings move so fast that they often appear blurred in photographs!

専門用語

- □ buzzing sound ブンブンという音

注

- □ up to 〜 「(時間・空間)(最高)〜まで、〜に至るまで」
- □ have stuffed themselves 「腹いっぱい食べた」
- ※ stuff oneself 「腹いっぱい食べる」
- □ feel like S V… 「…のように感じる」
- □ appear blurred 「ぼやけて見える」
- ※ appear + 形容詞(分詞)で、「…のように見える」
- ※ blur 「ぼんやりさせる」

Topic.15

How many types of volcanoes are there and what are they?

Steve Mattox, a volcanologist (someone who studies volcanoes), says that there are twenty-six different types of volcanoes! The most common types are stratovolcanoes, shield volcanoes, submarine volcanoes, volcanic fields, cinder cones, and calderas. A volcano is any vent in the surface of the Earth through which magma (hot melted rock!) erupts. While volcanoes are usually shaped like a cone, they can also look just like a hole in the ground.

専門用語

- ☐ volcanologist　火山学者　☐ stratovolcano　成層火山
- ☐ shield volcano　盾状火山　☐ submarine volcano　海底火山
- ☐ volcanic field　火山群
- ☐ cinder cone　スコリア丘
- ☐ caldera　カルデラ

注

火山の分類について

昔は火山の地形だけで分類するのが普通だった。

例えばコニーデ、トロイデといった分類である。ただ, 現在では、火山の地形だけでは、その火山の成り立ちを必ずしも反映していないことがわかってきて、内部構造に注目した、成層火山、盾状火山などの用語が使われるのが一般的である。

※stratovolcanoは成層火山。粘性がやや高く、爆発的噴火による熱いマグマのしぶき（火砕物）の割合が多いため、溶岩と火砕物の互層からなる傾斜の大きな山体を持つ火山です。成層火山はスコリア丘(scoria cone, cinder cone)や溶岩ドーム(lava dome)などを火山体全体として含むことが多い。富士山や三宅島など日本の火山の大部分はこの成層火山である。

※shield volcanoは、盾状火山。粘性の低い、あまり爆発的噴火をしないマグマが、主に溶岩となって重なり、傾斜が緩やかな山体を作った火山を言う。典型例はハワイ。

※calderaはカルデラで、噴火や崩壊でできた大きな火口状地形のこと。

- [ ] vent in the surface of the Earth 「地球の表面にある抜け口」
- [ ] erupt 「(火山が)爆発する、噴火する、(感情などが)どっと出る」
- [ ] be shaped like a cone 「円錐形のような形をしている」

How do shells grow?

 Many animals with shells are born with a small shell. Over time as the animal gets older, its shell grows bigger. Shelled animals get calcium carbonate and other minerals from the water and food they eat. They have special organs that turn these minerals into shell material that the animal secretes in layers. An oyster makes a pearl in the same way as it makes its own shell – many layers of minerals are laid on top of each other. Hermit crabs are unusual because they live in shells, but they don't grow their own. Instead, they find an empty shell and move in. Sometimes they kick out another animal and live in its shell!

専門用語
- [ ] calcium carbonate　炭酸カルシウム
- [ ] secrete　〈器官が〉…を分泌する
- [ ] oyster　牡蠣(カキ)、真珠貝　　[ ] hermit crab　ヤドカリ

注
- [ ] over time 「長い間に、長い期間をかけて、時間がたてば」
- [ ] as the animal gets older 「その動物が大きくなるにつれて」
- [ ] turn these minerals into shell material
　　「これらのミネラルを貝殻の材料に変える」
- [ ] shell material that the animal secretes in layers
　　「その動物が分泌して(結果的に)層状になる貝殻の材料」
- [ ] in the same way as it makes its own shell
　　「自分自身の貝殻を作るのと同じ方法で」

Can you get milk from sheep?

Sure you can, and I hear it's not baaaaaaad! People around the world have raised sheep for milk, meat, and wool for hundreds of years. Certain types of cheeses are traditionally made from sheep's milk. According to CheeseNet, Greek cheeses like Feta are often made from sheep's milk. Roquefort cheese is a blue cheese that is also made from sheep's milk. These cheeses get a unique flavor from sheep's milk.

|専門用語|
- ☐ baaaaaad　(回答者が子供向けにふざけて羊の鳴き声のまねをしたもの) = bad
- ☐ Feta　フェタチーズ
- ☐ Roquefort　ロクフォール・チーズ(フランス産。熟成期間が短い羊のチーズの一種で、青かびチーズの代表的なもの)

|注|
- ☐ blue cheese　「ブルーチーズ(青かびが縞状になっているチーズ)」

What is a vaccine?

A vaccine is a medicine that protects you from serious diseases like polio and measles. Vaccines are made from a tiny piece of a weak or dead germ that causes the disease. This makes your body create defensive cells called antibodies that will fight off the disease. Once you get a vaccine, you are immune from that disease. Vaccination programs have saved lives around the world and have made some deadly diseases very rare. Vaccines are usually given by a shot. It can hurt a little, but it's over really fast. The best thing about vaccines and shots – aside from keeping you healthy – is that you need fewer of them as you get older!

|専門用語|

☐ vaccine　ワクチン　☐ antibody　抗体

|注|

> ワクチンとは、接種して感染症の予防に用いる医薬品のこと。
> 弱い病原菌により体内に抗体を作り、以後感染症にかかりにくくする。弱いといっても病原菌を接種するため、まれに体調が崩れることもある。なお、ワクチンを発見したのはイギリスの医学者、エドワード・ジェンナーである。彼は牛痘にかかった人間は天然痘にかからなくなる（またはかかっても症状が軽い）事を発見し、これにより天然痘ワクチンを作った。
> ワクチンは生ワクチンと不活化ワクチンに分類することができる。生ワクチンは、弱った微生物（本文中のweak germ）を使用するもの。不活化ワクチンは死ワクチンとも呼ばれ、化学処理などによって死んだウィルス、細菌（本文中のdead germ）を使用するもの。生ワクチンより副作用が少ないが、その分免疫の続く期間が短いことがある。

☐ polio　「ポリオ、小児麻痺」　☐ measles　「はしか」
☐ fight off　「戦って撃退する、寄せつけない」
☐ Once you get a vaccine, you are immune from that disease.
　「ひとたびワクチンを接種すれば、あなたはその病気に対して免疫を持つようになる」
※このonceは接続詞。be immune from ～「～に対する免疫があって」
☐ vaccination program　「ワクチン接種計画」
☐ hurt　「(体の部分が)痛む、(注射などが)痛みを与える」。ここでは自動詞。
☐ shot　「皮下注射、ワクチン接種」
☐ it's over really fast　「すぐに終わる」

Where do cashews come from?

Topic.19

　Cashews grow on trees in tropical areas near the Equator. In Brazil, for instance, they grow in the wild! There are also many cashew farms in India. Cashew trees grow to the size of apple trees, and are often mistaken for bushes because their branches hang low to the ground. Sometimes these branches go into the ground and replant themselves! Cashews from Brazil are large and soft, while cashews from India are smaller and harder.

|専門用語|

☐ bush　潅木　☐ replant oneself　植え替わる

Where do cashews come from?

注

- [ ] be mistaken for 〜　「〜と間違えられる」
- [ ] their branches hang low to the ground
  「枝は地面の方に向かって低く垂れ下がる」
- [ ] go into the ground and replant themselves
  「地面の中へ入っていって、植え替わる」。カシューにかぎらず、一般的に木の枝の一部を地面にうめておくと、その部分から根が発生することが多い。根が発生した部分の両側を切断すると、それが新たに一本の木になるわけだ。このような技術を、「取り木」と呼んでいる。

How old is the Earth?

The Earth is about four and a half billion years old! The Earth began as a large cloud of dust and gas in space, which gradually collapsed together. The force of gravity that caused this collapse made the Earth very, very hot. It eventually cooled and expelled lots of gas into space, which was the beginning of our atmosphere. Water vapor from these gases fell back down to Earth and created our first oceans.

専門用語

- [ ] water vapor　水蒸気

注

- [ ] four and a half billion　「45億」
- [ ] cloud　「(ほこり・煙・蒸気などの)雲状のもの」
- [ ] collapsed together　「互いに結合してしぼんで行った」
- ※ collapseという動詞は、「崩壊する」という意味が一般的だが、ここでは、「(風船など、それまで膨張していたものの膨張状態が崩壊するという意味から)しぼむ」という意味である。

How many teeth does an adult have?

An adult human has thirty-two teeth. Most people start getting their baby teeth around the age of six months, and then they lose them as their permanent teeth grow in starting around the age of seven. Your baby teeth are important – they help guide the adult teeth into the proper position. You have different teeth for different jobs – incisors for biting, canines for grabbing, and molars for chewing. It's important to brush and floss every day, so you can keep your chompers pearly white and free from cavities.

|専門用語|

- □ incisor　門歯　□ canine　犬歯　□ grab　～をつかむ
- □ molar　臼歯　□ floss　(歯をデンタル)フロスできれいにする
- □ chompers　歯

|注|

- □ baby teeth　「乳歯」
- □ permanent teeth　「永久歯」
- □ grow in　「内側へ伸びる」
- □ help (to) guide the adult teeth into the proper position
  「永久歯が正しい場所にはえてくるように導くのに役立つ」
- □ grab ～　「～をつかむ」
- □ so (that) you can keep your chompers pearly white and (you can keep your chompers) free from cavities
  「あなたの歯が真珠のような白色に輝き続け、虫歯から免れることができるように」

※ so that S can … 構文である。この構文でthat が抜けるのは口語的。

参考HP　http://www.kyouseisika.info/1_6.html

Do fish drink water?

What a clever question! The answer is that fish do drink water – all animals (including ourselves) need water to survive. They also extract oxygen from water in order to breathe. But what about fish that swim in the ocean? Do they drink salt water? Yes, but saltwater fish excrete a lot of salt with the help of their gills. That's why most fish taste surprisingly unsalty.

専門用語
- □ excrete　〜を排泄する　□ gill　えら

注
- □ fish do drink water 「魚は本当に水を飲むんだよ」
- ※ 述語動詞の前に強調のdoを入れた形。「本当に…する、まさに…する」
- □ extract oxygen from water in order to breathe
  「呼吸をするために水から酸素を抽出する」
- ※ in order to do 「…するために」
- □ What about 〜? 「〜についてはどうだろう」
- □ That's why most fish taste surprisingly unsalty.
  「そういうわけでほとんどの魚は驚くほど塩辛くないんだ」
- ※ That's why S V… 「そういうわけで…だ」
- ※ taste + 形容詞 ＝「…の味がする」
- ※ unsaltyは形容詞 salty(塩辛い)に、反対の意味を表す接頭辞un- が付いたもの。

How old is the Great Barrier Reef?

It's very difficult to tell how old it is, because the Great Barrier Reef is actually a huge collection of hundreds of different kinds of corals. The world's largest reef probably took several thousand years to develop to its current size. Located off the northeast coast of Australia, the Great Barrier Reef is actually a collection of over 2,800 reefs. Corals are tiny animals that build large skeletons to survive. They can grow up to three inches a day.

専門用語
- coral　サンゴ　☐ reef　（さんご）礁　☐ skeleton　骨格(構造)

注
- the Great Barrier Reef　「グレート・バリア・リーフ」。オーストラリアにあり、ユネスコの世界遺産に登録されている。
- took several thousand years to develop to its current size
「現在の大きさに発達するのに数千年かかった」
- Located off the northeast coast of Australia
「オーストラリアの北東海岸の沖にあって」。分詞構文である

※ be located　「位置する」
※ off 〜　「〜の沖合いに」
- a collection of over 2,800 reefs　「2,800以上のサンゴ礁の集合体」
- up to three inches a day　「一日あたり、3インチまで」

※ up to 〜　「(時間的・空間的に)(最高)〜まで」

Topic.24

Who is the tallest person ever?

According to Guinness World Records, the tallest person ever recorded was a man named Robert Pershing Wadlow, who was eight feet and 11.1 inches tall!　He was born in Alton, Illinois and died in 1940. He wasn't just tall – he was big all over. On his 21st birthday, he weighed over 490 pounds! As a kid, he was so strong, he could carry his own father up the stairs of their house. The tallest people currently alive are a Tunisian man, Radhouane Charbib, who is seven feet and 8.9 inches tall, and an Indiana woman, Sandy Allen, who is seven feet and seven inches tall. To meet a whole bunch of tall people, you might visit the Tutsi tribe of Rwanda and Burundi in Central Africa. Adult Tutsi men average six feet tall.

専門用語
- Guinness World Records
「Guinness Book of World Records(ギネスブック)に登録されている記録」
- Tunisian　チュニジアの

Who is the tallest person ever?

注

- [ ] the tallest person ever recorded
  「今までに記録されているもっとも背の高い人」
- [ ] a man named ～　「～という名前の人」
- [ ] eight feet and 11.1 inches
  → 8×30.48 cm + 11.1×2.54 cm = 272 cm
- [ ] Alton, Illinois　「アメリカ合衆国イリノイ州のオールトン」
- [ ] He wasn't just tall　「彼は背が高いだけではなかった」
- [ ] all over　「全体にわたって」
- [ ] 490 pounds → 490×0.454 kg = 222.5 kg
- [ ] The tallest people currently alive
  「現在生きているもっとも背の高い人」
- [ ] an Indiana woman, Sandy Allen
  「インディアナ州の女性のSandy Allen」
- [ ] a whole bunch of ～　「非常にたくさんの～」
- [ ] you might visit ～　「～を訪問してはいかがでしょう」
※ このmightは、軽い命令・依頼・提案などを表し、「…してくださいませんか、…してはどうでしょう」。
(例) You might pass me the newspaper, please.
(すみませんが新聞を取っていただけませんか。)なお、この意味ではmayは用いない。
- [ ] the Tutsi tribe of Rwanda and Burundi in Central Africa
  「中央アフリカのルワンダやブルンジに住むツチ族」
- [ ] average six feet tall　「平均すると6フィートだ」
※ このaverageは動詞。

Why are primary colors called primary?

The colors red, blue, and green are called primary colors because by mixing just these three colors you can create all the colors in the spectrum. Most of the colors that you see are mixtures of two or more colors. The word "primary" is an adjective used to describe anything that occurs first, or is most important. It makes sense that we call these colors primary, since all other colors come from them!

注

☐ primary color　原色
※「色の3原色」は、赤黄青であり、「光の3原色」は、赤緑青である点に注意。ここでは、「光の3原色」について述べられている。
☐ all the colors in the spectrum　「スペクトル中のすべての色」
☐ The word "primary" is an adjective (which is) used to describe 〜
　「"primary" という言葉は、〜を言い表すために使われる形容詞である」
☐ It makes sense that S V…　「…ということは道理にかなう、意味がある」

参考HP　http://www.laser.phys.tohoku.ac.jp/~yoshi/hikari22.html

Topic.26

Why are cats afraid of water?

Not all cats are afraid of water. In fact, cat species that live in hot areas enjoy water. Tigers, lions, jaguars, ocelots, and jaguarundi all live in hot savannas, and they like taking dips in cool, refreshing streams and ponds. But cats from cold areas don't like the wet stuff that much. Snow leopards, lynx, bobcats, and cougars live in cold places, so they don't want to get wet. Water could make their fur less able to keep out the cold. Also, no cat wants to be splashed with water or dunked into a bath.

専門用語

☐ jaguar　ジャガー
☐ ocelot　オセロット（米国 Texas 州から南米にかけて産する斑点模様のあるヒョウに似た野生ネコの一種）
☐ jaguarundi　ジャガランディ（アメリカ合衆国から南アメリカに分布する。体長は50〜78cm）
☐ savanna　サバンナ　　☐ snow leopard　ユキヒョウ
☐ lynx　オオヤマネコ　　☐ bobcat　ボブキャット
☐ cougar　クーガー
☐ dunk　（水に）ちょっとつける

Topic.26
Why are cats afraid of water?

注

- ☐ Not all cats are afraid of water.
  「すべてのネコが水をこわがるわけではない」。部分否定に注意。
- ☐ in fact 「実際に、(だが)実は」
- ☐ cat species 「ネコ科の動物」
- ☐ take a dip 「(液などに)ちょっとつかる」
- ☐ cats from cold areas don't like the wet stuff that much.
  「寒冷な地域のネコ科動物は水をそれほど好まない」
- ※ stuff 「材料、(ばくぜんと)もの」。wet stuff(湿ったもの)とはすなわち水のこと。
- ※ not … that much 「それほど…でない」。このthatは副詞。
- ☐ get wet 「水に濡れる」
- ☐ Water could make their fur less able to keep out the cold.
  「水に濡れると毛皮は寒さを締め出しにくくなるだろう」
- ※ このcouldは仮定法を作るためのもの。「…という可能性があるだろう」くらいの意味である。仮定法はif節がなくてもよい。
- ☐ splash 「(水・泥を)はねかける」

Topic.27
What is genetic engineering?

Genetic engineering is when scientists modify DNA and other genetic materials. DNA is short for deoxyribonucleic acid, and it's the blueprint for living things. DNA determines whether you have blue or brown eyes or if a tomato is bright red or green. Scientists can make some small changes in animals and plants by altering DNA. They've made new drugs to help sick people and modified food plants to grow bigger and resist diseases. Some people are worried that genetic engineering of foods isn't healthy for the environment, and that cloning could lead to ethical problems.

専門用語

- ☐ genetic engineering 遺伝子工学、遺伝子操作
- ☐ DNA

- ☐ deoxyribonucleic acid
  デオキシリボ核酸(主に細胞核に染色体として存在する遺伝子の本体)

> 注

- ☐ Genetic engineering is (the engineering) when scientists modify DNA and other genetic materials. このように補ってみる。
- ☐ modify DNA 「DNAを部分的に変更する」
- ☐ DNA and other genetic materials
  「DNAやその他の遺伝物質」
- ☐ be short for 〜 「〜を略したものだ」
- ☐ the blueprint for living things
  「生物にとっての設計図」
- ☐ DNA determines whether you have blue or brown eyes or (DNA determines) if a tomato is bright red or green.
  「DNAはあなたが青い目を持つのか茶色の目を持つのかを決定する。あるいは、あるトマトの色が明るい赤なのか緑なのかを決定する」
- ※ ifは接続詞で、「…かどうか」
- ☐ make some small changes 「小さな変更を加える」
- ☐ by altering DNA
  「DNAを部分的に変えることによって」
- ☐ modify food plants to grow bigger and resist diseases
  「野菜(のDNA)に部分的な変更を加えてより大きくしたり、病気に対して抵抗力を持つようにする」
- ☐ be worried that S V… 「…ということで心配する」
- ☐ genetic engineering of foods
  「食材に遺伝子操作を加えること」
- ☐ cloning could lead to ethical problems
  「クローニングは倫理上の問題を引き起こす可能性があるだろう」
- ※ lead to 〜 「〜を引き起こす」= bring about 〜

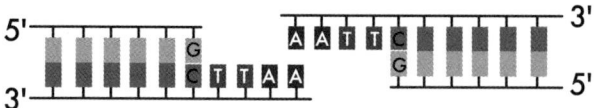

How did the planets get their names?

The five planets closest to Earth were known since ancient times. Mercury, Venus, Mars, Jupiter, and Saturn were all named in ancient Rome after the Roman gods and goddesses. Most of the names fit pretty well. Mars was the Roman god of war who loved bloody battles, and the planet Mars looks red like blood. Jupiter was the king of the Roman gods, and Jupiter is the biggest of all the planets. In 1781, Sir William Herschel discovered Uranus, and he debated with other astronomers about what to name the planet. Finally, everyone agreed to stick with ancient Roman and Greek names. The next planets to be discovered, Neptune and Pluto, were also named after ancient gods.

専門用語

- □ bloody battle 　血なまぐさい戦争　□ Uranus　天王星
- □ Neptune　海王星　□ Pluto　冥王星

注

- □ ancient times　「古代」
- □ Mercury, Venus, Mars, Jupiter, and Saturn
   順に、「水星、金星、火星、木星、土星」
- □ in ancient Rome　「古代ローマ時代に」。be named after ～(～にちなんで名づけられる)に、割り込んでいる形。
- □ fit pretty well　「かなりよく合致する」
- □ what to name the planet　「その惑星にどんな名前をつけるべきか」
- □ stick with ～　「～を固執する」
※ 前置詞はwithの他にto、byなどを取る。

参考

天王星には27個の衛星がある。
他の惑星では、その衛星の名前もやはり古代ローマやギリシアの名前にちなんでつけられているが、天王星は例外で、シェークスピアなどの作品に登場する人物の名前が付けられたという。
http://www.izu.co.jp/~at-sushi/astro/

Why is a banana a fruit? Where are the seeds?

Topic.29

A fruit is the ripened ovary of a plant, and it holds the plant's seeds. Fruits grow from a plant's flowers, and bananas do all of these things! Banana plants have flowering stems, and when the flowers mature, the ovaries inside them become bananas. In some types of banana, you can see very tiny seeds right in the center of the fruit. But many of the bananas you get at the grocery store are purposefully made to be seedless. Specialty stores sell banana seeds so you can grow your own plants. Banana plantations grow new plants by taking a fleshy bulb called a rhizome off an old plant, and then planting the rhizome.

専門用語
- ovary　子房　□ fleshy bulb　多肉質の鱗茎　□ rhizome　地下茎

注
- banana plant　「バナナの木」
- flowering stem　「ここでは花房(花が咲く茎の一部)」
- right in the center of the fruit　「その果物のちょうど真ん中に」
  ※ rightは副詞で、「ちょうど」
- grocery store　「食料品店」
- are purposefully made to be seedless　「故意に種無しにされている」
- specialty store　「専門店(ここでは種苗専門店)」
- banana plantation　「バナナ園」

> **Banana plantations grow new plants by taking a fleshy bulb called a rhizome off an old plant, and then (banana plantations grow new plants by) planting the rhizome.**
> 「バナナ園では成長したバナナの木から地下茎と呼ばれている多肉質の鱗茎を切り離し、その地下茎を植えるという作業によって、次の世代のバナナの木を育てている」。「バナナ園」は、正確にいうとバナナ栽培の専門家のことであろう。この一文は、バナナ農園がどのようにしてバナナの木をふやしているのかを説明したもの。つまり、種子を蒔くことによってふやすのではなくて、地下茎の部分を分割することによって新しいバナナの木を育成しているわけである。an old plant(古いバナナの木)というのは、「新しいバナナの木」に対して用いた表現であって、バナナの木が古くなっているわけではない。(なお参考までに)ある植物が、「野菜なのか果物なのか」の定義はかなり複雑で、国によってもその境界線があいまいである。各自調べてみると面白い。

Who invented the telescope?

The telescope is a result of experimenting with lenses in Europe during the 15th and 16th centuries. Many people were involved, and nobody is sure who first invented the telescope. In 1608, several men in the Netherlands applied for telescope patents or showed a telescope at fairs. The first was Hans Lipperhey, but his patent application was denied because the telescope was too easy to copy. The next year, astronomer Galileo Galilei made his own telescope and improved on the earlier designs. He pointed his telescope to the skies to discover four of Jupiter's moons and make new observations about the Moon, Sun, and the motion of planets and stars. While Galileo didn't invent the telescope, he did make it popular!

注

- □ nobody is sure who first invented the telescope.
  「だれが最初に望遠鏡を発明したかについては、だれにもわからない」
- □ the Netherlands 「オランダ」
- □ applied for telescope patents
  「望遠鏡に関する特許を申請した」
- □ at fairs 「博覧会(見本市)で」
- □ patent application 「特許の申請」
- □ the telescope was too easy to copy
  「その望遠鏡は複製品を作ると言えないほど簡単な作りだった」。つまり特許申請の価値がないほど簡単な作りだったわけである。
- □ improved on the earlier designs 「初期のデザインに改良を加えた」
- □ pointed his telescope to the skies to discover ～
  「自分の望遠鏡を空に向けて～を発見した」。この不定詞は、「結果を表す不定詞」
- □ four of Jupiter's moons 「木星の衛星のうちの4つ」

> 木星には63個の衛星がある。ガリレオ衛星と呼ばれる4大衛星(イオ、エウロパ、ガニメデ、カリスト)とアマルテアを除く他の衛星はすべて20世紀になって発見された。なお、四大衛星のうちのエウロパの氷地殻の下には海洋が存在し、生命が存在している可能性が高いと期待されている。

□ motion of planets and stars 「惑星や恒星の動き」
□ he did make it popular 「彼はそれを普及させた」
※ did は強調を表す。he made it popular の強調形。

How many species of pandas are there?

Topic.31

Only two species of pandas exist in the world, and scientists aren't positive they are related! The red panda was first identified by Europeans in 1821. The name "panda" was modified from a Chinese name for the small, red, raccoon-like animal. But in 1869, Europeans encountered a large, black and white, bear-like animal in China. They called this the giant panda because it only ate bamboo, just like the red panda. Both animals live in the mountains of China and both are rare today. But these animals have a lot of differences, and scientists still don't know if the animals are biologically related.

専門用語
□ red panda アカパンダ (レッサーパンダ)
□ raccoon-like アライグマによく似た

注
□ scientists aren't positive they are related
「科学者は2種類のパンダが関係があるのかどうかについて確信が持てない」
※ be positive about 〜, be positive that …
(〜を確信する、…であることを確信する)
□ The name "panda" was modified from a Chinese name for the small, red, raccoon-like animal.
「"panda"という名前は、その小さくて赤く、アライグマによく似た動物につけられた中国語の名前を部分的に修正したものだ」

参考HP
http://hy4477u.hp.infoseek.co.jp/doubutubetu/sonota/resapanda/resapanda009.jpg

28

Topic.32

How long would it take to get to Pluto?

Pluto is the farthest planet from our sun, and it has a weird orbit that takes the planet as far as 4.6 billion miles away from the sun and as close as 2.7 billion miles. NASA has plans to send an unmanned spacecraft to Pluto. The New Horizons Pluto Kuiper Belt Flyby is planned to launch in January 2006, and it should reach Pluto in the summer of 2015 or 2016. So that's nine or ten years to get from Earth to Pluto!

専門用語

□ Pluto 冥王星

注

冥王星は1930年に発見された、太陽系のいちばん外側を回る惑星。247.8年という長い時間をかけて太陽のまわりを公転する。直径約2300キロメートル。そのまわりを直径1200キロメートルの衛星「カロン」が回っている。

冥王星の大きな特徴は公転軌道であるが、それは他の惑星とは大きく異なる。だ円を描き、ほかの惑星の軌道に比べて約17度も傾いている。そのため、太陽から最も離れているときは74億キロメートル、いちばん近いときには44億キロメートルになる。極端なだ円を描くので、1979年〜1999年の間は海王星の軌道より内側に入っていた。

□ the farthest planet 「最も遠い惑星」
※ farthest は far の最上級。
□ weird orbit 「不可思議な軌道」
□ unmanned spacecraft 「無人の宇宙船」

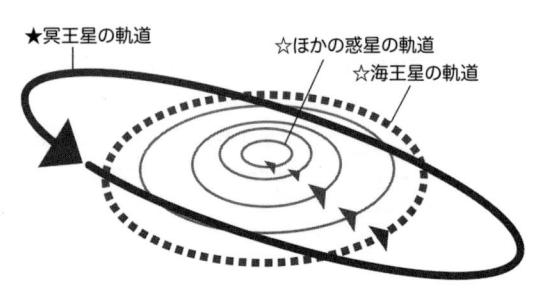

★冥王星の軌道
☆ほかの惑星の軌道
☆海王星の軌道

What do male mosquitoes eat?

I guess you already know that female mosquitoes are the ones that bite you and me (ouch!) and suck our blood. The female needs the protein in a blood meal for her eggs. But what does the guy eat? Male mosquitoes drink nectar from flowers and juices from plants. Pretty sweet, huh? Actually, in some species of mosquitoes, both females and males eat nectar and juice, and the females only drink blood when they're going to lay eggs. If you live in an area that mosquitoes seem to like, take care and try not to get bit this summer!

注

- [ ] the ones that bite you and me (ouch!) and suck our blood
  「君や私を刺して(いたい！)私たちの血を吸う蚊」
- [ ] protein in a blood meal
  「血の食事の中にあるタンパク質」。人の血液を食事にたとえている。
- [ ] guy　ここでは、「オスの蚊」のこと。
- [ ] nectar from flowers　「花の蜜」
- [ ] juices from plants
  「植物の液(たとえば樹液)」
- [ ] Pretty sweet, huh?
  「けっこう甘いんじゃないの？」
- [ ] Actually, in some species of mosquitoes, both females and males eat nectar and juice, and the females only drink blood when they're going to lay eggs.
  「実は、オスもメスも花の蜜や植物の液を常食とするが、メスは産卵をしようとするときに(人の)血だけを吸うという種類の蚊もいる」
- [ ] lay eggs　「卵を産む、産卵する」
- [ ] try not to …　「…しないように(努力)する」
- [ ] get bit　「(蚊に)刺される」

What is the most popular flavor of ice cream?

Topic.34

According to supermarket sales, vanilla is the number one flavor of ice cream in the U.S., and it's one of the oldest and most popular flavors of all time. After vanilla, chocolate is a distant second place, and then nut flavors like butter pecan are third most popular. I'm a big fan of chocolate myself. What flavor of ice cream do you scream for?

専門用語
- pecan　ペカンの実(食用)

注
- supermarket sales 「スーパーの売り上げ(高)」
- distant second place 「第一位とかなり離された第二位」
- butter pecan 「バターペカン」。バターとペカンナッツ。
- What flavor of ice cream do you scream for?
  「君はアイスクリームのどの味を求めてきゃっきゃっ声をあげるの？」
※ この返答には、I scream for 〜が予想される。つまり、ice cream for〜との掛け言葉。

参考HP: http://aggie-horticulture.tamu.edu/extension/homefruit/pecan/pecan.html

Who invented electricity?

Topic.35

Well, no one really "invented" electricity, but you can ask who discovered it. While people have known about the powerful effects of lightning for thousands of years, the first person to discover that lightning was a naturally occurring form of electricity was Benjamin Franklin. In 1752, during a dangerous electrical storm, Franklin flew a kite that had a metal key at the bottom of the string. When a bolt of lightning hit the kite, a spark of electricity flew from the key! From this experiment, Franklin invented the lightning rod, which attracts lightning and draws it into the ground. This saves many buildings from burning down.

専門用語
- flow a kite　凧を揚げる

注
- the first person to discover that lightning was a naturally occurring form of electricity was Benjamin Franklin.
「稲妻は自然に発生する電気の一つの形態だということを発見した最初の人はベンジャミン・フランクリンだった」
※ that から electricity までは名詞節でdiscoverの目的語。
※ the first person to…は、「…した最初の人」。不定詞の形容詞的用法。
※ electricityの後ろのwasはこの文全体の述語動詞。Benjamin Franklinは、その補語。
- naturally occurring form of electricity
「自然に発生する電気の一つの形態」
- a metal key at the bottom of the string
「その糸の最も低い位置には金属の鍵(がついていた)」。ここでは鍵がポイントなのではなくて、金属がポイント。

Why does salt water exist?

Topic.36

The salt in salt water comes from the Earth. Salt is a mineral, and is stored in deposits both on land and under the water. When rivers run to the ocean, they accumulate all kinds of minerals, including salt, and deposit them into the ocean. Salt dissolves easily into water, which means it is a solvent. However, salt cannot evaporate with water into the atmosphere, so the level of salt in the oceans has been slowly building over the years! The salt in ocean water also comes from deposits under the sea floor.

Why does salt water exist?　　　　　　　　　　　　　　Topic.36

[専門用語]
- □ solvent　溶媒(溶液をつくるとき、溶質をとかす液体)
- □ the level of salt　塩分の濃度
- □ has been slowly building　ゆっくりと高まった
- □ deposits under the sea floor　海底の下にある塩層

[注]
- □ and (salt) is stored in deposits both on land and under the water
  「陸や水中の堆積層の中に貯蔵されている」
- □ under the water　「水中の」
- ※ 前置詞 under には、「〜の下に」という基本的な意味の他に、「(覆い包む物)の中に、の内部に」という意味もある。
  なお、塩層としてはボリビアのUyuni Salt Depositが有名。
- □ accumulate all kinds of minerals, including salt
  「塩分も含めて、あらゆる種類のミネラルを(一箇所に)集める」。ミネラルは川の水の中にあって、常に流されている時には蓄積する機会がないが、ひとたび海に出れば、川の水の場合ほど常に流れるということはないのだから、「蓄積」ということが起こりうる。
- □ deposit them into the ocean
  「それら(あらゆる種類のミネラル)を海洋に向かって送り込んでいく」
  http://www.comunidadandina.org/ingles/tourism/greatest/salt_uyuni.htm
- □ ,which means it is a solvent
  「それは水が(塩分の)溶媒だということだ」。,whichの先行詞は前文の内容(つまり、「塩分は水に容易に溶ける」ということ)

[参考]
「海水はなぜ塩辛いのか？」に対する完璧な答はまだ確立していないようだ。地球が形成された当時、地表は一時的に塩酸の海だった。塩酸は岩石層を溶かし、そこから流出したNa^+イオンと塩酸中のCl^-イオンとが大量のNacl(塩)を作り現在に至るとする説もある。

参考HP
- http://www.geolab.jp/ms-science/science14.html#page_top
- http://ga.water.usgs.gov/edu/whyoceansalty.html
- http://www.utdallas.edu/~pujana/oceans/why.html
- http://www.shiop.co.jp/monoshio/kagaku/main.htm

What percentage of people are lefties?

Topic.37

About ten percent of the population is left-handed. Some people are equally comfortable using their left or right hand – they are called ambidextrous. Did you know that the right side of the brain controls muscles on the left side of the body, and the left side of the brain controls muscles on the right? People also tend to favor one foot, or eye, or ear!

専門用語
☐ ambidextrous　両手が利く

注
☐ Some people are equally comfortable using their left or right hand
「左手を使っても右手を使っても同じように快適な人もいる」

Why do we sneeze?

Topic.38

Sneezing is the body's way of getting rid of irritants in the nose and mouth region. Sneezing can be caused by lots of things, including dust, tree pollen, and mildew. Some people sneeze when they are exposed to bright light! They are called photic sneezers, and they inherit this trait from their parents. If you are allergic to something, you'll often sneeze. This is simply your body reacting to something that it wants out! When you sneeze you use all kinds of muscles, including your stomach, diaphragm, chest, and throat.

専門用語
☐ irritant　刺激物　☐ the nose and mouth region　鼻や口の部位
☐ mildew　白かび　☐ photic sneezer　光刺激によってくしゃみをする人
☐ diaphragm　横隔膜

Why do we sneeze?

Topic.38

注
- the body's way of getting rid of irritants
  「身体が刺激物を取り除く方法」
- ※ get rid of 〜　「〜を取り除く」
- □ tree pollen　「木々の花粉」
- □ are exposed to 〜　「〜にさらされる」
- □ be allergic to 〜　「〜にアレルギーを起こして」
- □ This is simply your body reacting to something that it wants out!
  「これは単にあなたの身体が、(身体から)出ていってほしいと思っているものに対して反応しているだけだ」
- ※ reactingは動名詞。your bodyは、その意味上の主語。「あなたの身体の反応」。

Topic.39

How long can a turtle stay underwater without coming up for air?

All turtles have lungs and must breathe air. Most sea turtles, the large turtles that swim for hundreds of miles every year, can stay underwater for as long as 45 minutes, but green sea turtles can stay submerged for up to five hours. Smaller turtles have to resurface more often. Some turtles can absorb oxygen through their skin, and are able to stay underwater for days while they are hibernating!

専門用語
- □ turtle　カメ(特にウミガメをいう)　□ green sea turtle　アオウミガメ
- □ stay submerged　水中にいる　□ resurface　再び浮上する

注

通常、turtlesは「ウミガメ」、淡水や陸のカメはtortoiseという。
ただし、この英文ではsea turtleという表現を用いていること、さらには一般にfreshwater turtle(淡水のカメ)という表現もあることから、本文一行目のturtleは、「カメ」と考えられる。

- ☐ stay underwater for as long as 45 minutes
  「水中に45分間もとどまることができる」
- ☐ up to five hours 　「5時間まで」
- ☐ Some turtles can absorb oxygen through their skin, and are able to stay underwater for days while they are hibernating!
  「カメの中には皮膚から酸素を吸収することができるものもいて、冬眠中には何日間も水中にいることができる」

参考HP http://www.delco.co.jp/designmuseum/muse-de-turtese/about-turtle/about-turtle.html

Who invented the game of volleyball?

Topic.40

An American named William G. Morgan invented the game of volleyball in 1895. Morgan was a YMCA instructor who decided to make up a whole new game using parts of basketball, baseball, tennis, and handball. He wanted it to be fun and active, but not as physical as basketball. At first he called it "mintonette," but then someone else suggested "volleyball."

専門用語
- ☐ mintonette 　ミントネット　☐ physical 　(スポーツで)行為が荒っぽい

注

バレーボールは、アメリカでウイリアム・G・モーガンとスプリングフィールド大学の学生、そしてマサチューセッツのYMCAのマネージャーによって「Mintonette(ミントネット)」の呼び名で1895年に発明された。バレーボールがオリンピック競技になったのは、1964年第18回東京大会のことで、この大会で優勝した日本チームは東洋の魔女と呼ばれ、その強さが世界に知られることになった。なお、volleyとは、「ボールが着地する前に打ったり蹴ったりすること」という意味。

- ☐ whole new 〜　「(それまでと違って)まったく新しい〜」

参考HP http://www.geocities.jp/volley344/his.html

Is there really trash up in space?

Topic.41

Unfortunately, yes. The 1,000 artificial satellites currently orbiting the Earth make up only 5% of the man-made objects in space. This space junk is mostly made up of dead satellites, discarded rocket stages, thousands of chunks smaller than 8 inches in diameter, and billions of really small bits. Most of this space debris will eventually fall back to Earth and burn up in the atmosphere.

[専門用語]
- □ trash　くず、がらくた　□ junk　くず、がらくた
- □ rocket stage　(多段式ロケットの)段(それぞれにタンクと燃料をもっている)
- □ chunk　かたまり　□ debris　破片

[注]
- □ artificial satellites currently orbiting the Earth
「現在地球の周りを軌道に乗って回っている人工衛星」
- □ make up ～　「～を構成する」
- □ man-made objects in space　「宇宙に存在する人工の物体」
- □ mostly　「たいていは、ほとんどの場合」。sometimes「時々」に対立する言葉。
- □ be made up of ～　「～から成り立っている」
- □ in diameter　「直径が」
- □ burn up　「燃え尽きる」

Why are flamingoes pink?

Topic.42

Flamingoes are pink because of the shrimp they eat! Chemicals inside the crustaceans (or shrimp) turn the feathers reddish. The colors of flamingoes range from dark red to bright pink. They eat like baleen whales − sucking in water and capturing the tiny shrimp inside a comb-like structure called lamellae.

専門用語
- shrimp　小エビ
- crustacean　甲殻類の動物（カニ・エビなど）＜crust
- baleen whale　ヒゲクジラ
- lamellae　(lamellaの複数形) ラメラ（薄板）

注
- turn the feathers reddish　「羽を赤みがかった色に変える」
- range from dark red to bright pink
  「範囲が暗い赤色から明るいピンクに及ぶ」。
cf. range from A to B　「範囲がAからBにまで及んでいる」
- They eat like baleen whales
  「フラミンゴはヒゲクジラのような食べ方をする」
※ eatは自動詞として、likeは前置詞として使われている。

参考

baleen whale ヒゲクジラについて。
上あごのヒゲで、オキアミ、小魚を濾して食べる大型のクジラ。ヒゲクジラには、シロナガス(blue whale)、コククジラ(gray whale)、ザトウクジラ(humpback whale)、ミンククジラ(minke whale)などがある。

- suck in water　「水を吸い込む」
- tiny shrimp　「小エビ」。ここではshrimpが集合的に使われている。
- comb-like structure　「クシのような（体の）組織」

How many days does it take to get to Mars?

Topic.43

It usually takes an unmanned spacecraft nine to eleven months to reach Mars from Earth. That's about 270 to 330 days, which is quite a long time! Scientists are trying to get that figure reduced to six months, so we can some day send people to Mars! Sending people to Mars would help us learn about what the Earth was like long ago. We may also find signs of life that existed many millions of years ago on Mars.

How many days does it take to get to Mars? Topic.43

注
- unmanned spacecraft 「無人の宇宙船」
- get that figure reduced to six months 「その数字を6か月に減らす」
※ 第5文型で動詞getに対して、目的語はthat figure、補語はreduced。
cf. reduce A to B 「AをBに減少させる」
- Sending people to Mars would help us learn 〜
  「火星へ人を送ることは、私たちが〜を知るのに役立つだろう」
- what the Earth was like
  「地球がどのようなものであったのか」
- We may also find signs of life
  「私たちはまた生命の痕跡を発見するかもしれない」

What is narcolepsy? Topic.44

It's defined as a disorder that causes people to uncontrollably fall asleep at any time for a few minutes. About 1 in every 1,000 people have narcolepsy. The problem may be genetic, and it can also be caused by head injury. Doctors treat narcoleptics with stimulants to keep them awake. Sometimes a good nap schedule can help too.

専門用語
- narcolepsy （睡眠発作・過眠症）
- narcoleptic　ナルコレプシー患者　　□ stimulant　刺激剤

注

> 参考【narcolepsy】ナルコレプシーの症状について
> 過剰な眠気があり、昼間も眠気に襲われるなどの睡眠障害が現れる。

- It's defined as 〜 「〜と定義される」
- disorder 「病気、不調」
- cause people to uncontrollably fall asleep
  「人が眠りに落ちるのを制御できなくさせる」
- at any time 「いついかなる時にも」

- ☐ 1 in every 1,000 people 「1000人あたり1人」
- ☐ The problem may be genetic
  「問題はこの病気が遺伝病だということだろう」
- ☐ head injury 「頭部の傷害」
- ☐ keep them awake 「患者を眠らせない」
- ☐ a good nap schedule can help
  「計画的にうまく昼寝をすることも役に立つだろう」

Topic.45

Are dolphins intelligent?

Scientists have studied dolphins for a long time, and they believe that dolphins are as intelligent as chimpanzees and dogs. Dolphins can learn to perform complex tasks through the use of repetition and rewards by trainers. Researchers at Hawaii's Dolphin Institute have even taught dolphins to understand a modified sign language with about 100 different hand signals.

専門用語

- ☐ sign language サインランゲージ（記号言語、身ぶり言語）

注

- ☐ learn to … 「（学習によって）…するようになる」
- ☐ perform complex tasks 「複雑な課題をこなす」
- ☐ the use of repetition and rewards by trainers
  「調教師たちが、反復とごほうびの原則を使うこと」
- ☐ teach dolphins to understand ～
  「イルカが～を理解するように教育する」
- ☐ modified sign language
  「修正されたサインランゲージ」。サインランゲージ（記号言語）は、実質的には手話を示すことが多い。

Topic.46
Why does a satellite need a thermal blanket?

A thermal blanket is the outside protective layer of a satellite that makes it look shiny. This blanket keeps the satellite warm in the cold and cool in the heat. Since they orbit outside of the Earth's protective atmosphere, satellites are exposed to both very cold and very warm temperatures (-120 to +180 degrees). The complex electronic systems inside the satellites would be fried or frozen without the thermal blanket.

|専門用語|
- [ ] thermal blanket　サーマルブランケット（ ≒ thermal insulator 断熱材）

|注|
- [ ] outside protective layer of a satellite
「人工衛星の外側の保護層」。その素材は超耐熱性樹脂ポリイミドなど。
- [ ] be exposed to 〜　「〜にさらされる」

Topic.47
Why do you have to brush your teeth?

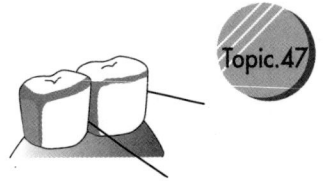

The short answer is that if you don't, your teeth might fall out. The slightly longer answer is that brushing your teeth gets rid of plaque. That is the stuff that builds up on your teeth and causes nasty cavities. Flossing every night also helps get rid of tartar, which is another mineral deposit that can send you to the dentist's office.

|専門用語|
- [ ] plaque　歯垢(しこう)(歯の表面に付着する白く柔らかい沈着物で、いわゆる細菌の固まり)　　☐ nasty　いやな　　☐ floss　デンタルフロスできれいにする
- [ ] tartar　歯石(プラーク(歯垢)が長い間歯についたままになっていると、唾液中のカルシウムなどが沈着して歯石になる

> 注
- □ if you don't ＝ if you don't brush your teeth
- □ your teeth might fall out 「あなたの歯は抜け落ちるかもしれない」
- □ slightly longer ＝ a little longer
- □ get rid of 〜 「〜を取り除く」
- □ stuff 「(漠然とした意味を表して)もの」
- □ build up on your teeth 「あなたの歯の上に蓄積する」
- □ cavity 「虫歯の穴、空洞」
- □ mineral deposit 「鉱物質(実際にはカルシウム)の層」

Why is some money on paper, and some in metal coins?

Topic.48

Early civilizations used shells, beads, and even grain to place value on goods. Coins and paper money were introduced by European settlers. Coins used to be made out of precious materials like gold or silver, so they had actual value. Paper was introduced as a way of representing large amounts of these coins. Today most countries use coins to denominate smaller amounts for practical reasons. You wouldn't want your wallet stuffed with five cent bills or fifty dollar coins!

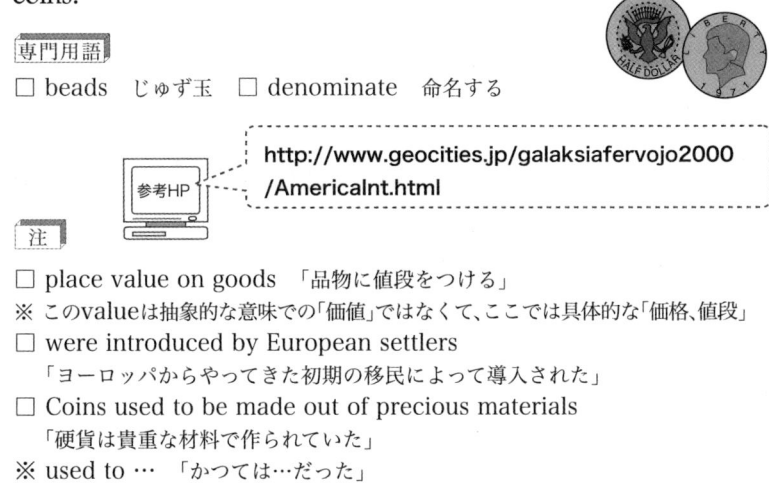

> 専門用語
- □ beads　じゅず玉　□ denominate　命名する

> 参考HP: http://www.geocities.jp/galaksiafervojo2000/Americalnt.html

> 注
- □ place value on goods 「品物に値段をつける」
- ※ このvalueは抽象的な意味での「価値」ではなくて、ここでは具体的な「価格、値段」
- □ were introduced by European settlers
   「ヨーロッパからやってきた初期の移民によって導入された」
- □ Coins used to be made out of precious materials
   「硬貨は貴重な材料で作られていた」
- ※ used to … 「かつては…だった」

42

Topic. 48

Why is some money on paper, and some in metal coins?
- [ ] actual value 「実際の価値(=貴金属そのものの価値)」
- [ ] large amounts of 〜 「大量の〜」
- [ ] represent 〜 「〜を表す、〜に相当する」
- [ ] denominate smaller amounts
  「小額(のお金)を表示する」。小額のお金であっても、独立した単位として使えるように命名するということ。
- [ ] practical reasons 「実用的な理由」
- [ ] You wouldn't want your wallet stuffed with five cent bills or fifty dollar coins!
  「あなたは自分の財布に5セント札とか50ドルコインなんかを詰め込みたくないよね(小額の紙幣とか高額のコインなんて実際的ではないよね)」
= You wouldn't want to stuff your wallet with five cent bills or fifty dollar coins!
※ stuff A with B 「AにBを詰め込む」

参考

アメリカで現在流通している紙幣とコインの種類。(2004年10月現在)
アメリカ・ドル(U.S.Dollar)。1.00ドル=100セント。
●紙幣の種類
1、2、5、10、20、50、100、500、1000、5000、10000の十一種類。
ただし、流通しているものは1、5、10、20ドル札で、たまに50、100ドル札も見かけるがニセ札でないかと確認されることがある。500ドル以上は流通していない。
●硬貨の種類
1セント(通称ペニーPenny)、5セント(ニッケルNickel)、10セント(ダイムDime)、25セント(クォーターQuarter)、50セント(ハーフダラHalf Dollar)、1ドル(ダラーコインDollar Coin)。50セントはあまり流通していない。

Topic.49

Who invented the dictionary?

Ever since civilizations started to write they made reference works that could be called early ancestors of the dictionary. The most famous of these is the Rosetta Stone, which was made in Egypt in 200 BC. It features an account of a king's crowning written in hieroglyphs, early Arabic, and Greek. It's closer to a translator's dictionary than a modern dictionary, but it's still a very important early reference work. Formal English dictionaries didn't appear until the early 17th century. Some of the more famous dictionaries were created by the Englishman Samuel Johnson in 1755, and the American Noah Webster in 1806.

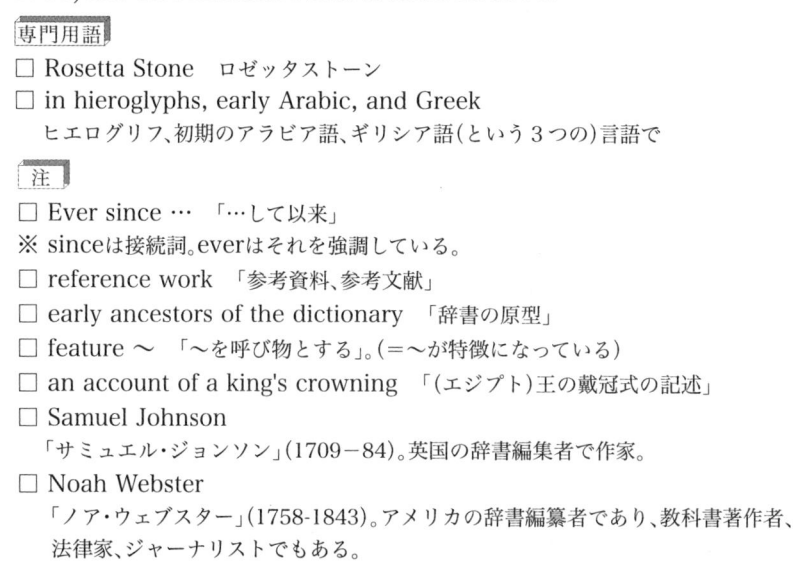

専門用語
- □ Rosetta Stone　ロゼッタストーン
- □ in hieroglyphs, early Arabic, and Greek
  ヒエログリフ、初期のアラビア語、ギリシア語（という３つの）言語で

注
- □ Ever since …　「…して以来」
  ※ sinceは接続詞。everはそれを強調している。
- □ reference work　「参考資料、参考文献」
- □ early ancestors of the dictionary　「辞書の原型」
- □ feature 〜　「〜を呼び物とする」。（＝〜が特徴になっている）
- □ an account of a king's crowning　「（エジプト）王の戴冠式の記述」
- □ Samuel Johnson
  「サミュエル・ジョンソン」(1709－84)。英国の辞書編集者で作家。
- □ Noah Webster
  「ノア・ウェブスター」(1758-1843)。アメリカの辞書編纂者であり、教科書著作者、法律家、ジャーナリストでもある。

参考【ロゼッタストーン】1799年８月、ナポレオンがエジプトを侵略したとき、ナイル川河口のロゼッタ村にある要塞の工事現場から、石碑の一部と思われる玄武岩が掘りだされ、発見地の名からロゼッタストーンと命名された。岩肌には３層にわかれて異なる文字が刻まれていた。最下段の文字は、すぐに読めた。内容は紀元前196年のエジプト王、プトレマイオス５世の戴冠式の知らせである。その時代のエジプトの王や貴族は、なんとギリシア文字を使っていたのだ。
その後、最上部の文字は、紀元前3000年ごろにできた王や神官が使った象形文字で、２段めは民衆文字であることがわかった。
最上段の文字は、ラテン語のヒエロ（神聖な）にグリフ（刻む）を合わせてヒエログリフとよばれ、民衆文字はデモティックとよばれた。この２種類の文字による碑文は、ギリシア文字と同じ内容を表していることもわかり、解読は時間の問題と思われた。しかし、この古代文字の謎を解くには、20年の歳月とひとりの天才ジャン・フランソワ・シャンポリオンを待たねばならなかった。

参考HP　http://www.labo-global.co.jp/spc-o-word/wordpro/rozetta.html

How is cheese made?

Topic.50

One legend tells of an Arab nomad who carried milk on a long, hard ride through the desert. The heat and the galloping of his horse turned the milk into cheese! Today, cheese is made by carefully warming milk until it separates into lumpy curds and liquid whey. A lactic starter and a rennet coagulating enzyme may be added to speed up the process. The curds can be used alone as cottage cheese. To make cheese like cheddar or Swiss, the curds are treated and pressed to remove all the whey. The cheese may then be ripened to get hard and improve the flavor.

専門用語

- □ nomad　遊牧民
- □ lumpy　でこぼこの　□ curd　凝乳
- □ whey　乳漿、乳清(チーズ製造で凝乳を除いた後に残る水のような液)
- □ lactic　乳の　□ starter　(機械の)起動装置
- □ rennet coagulating enzyme
  レニット凝固酵素(ミルクを凝固させるレニン酵素renninを含む)
- □ cottage cheese　カッテージ・チーズ(作ったばかりのソフト・チーズの一種)
- □ cheddar　チェダー・チーズ(長期間成熟して風味を増したハード・チーズの一種)
- □ Swiss (cheese)　スイス・チーズ(長期間成熟して風味を増したハード・チーズの一種)

注

- □ tell of 〜　「〜を物語る」
- □ on a ride　「乗り物に乗って」。この場合には、「馬に乗せて」
- □ The heat and the galloping of his horse
  「暑さと馬の疾走」。馬の疾走によって結果的にミルクが振動することをさす。
- □ turn A into B　「AをBに変える」
- □ lactic starter　starterは「(機械の)起動装置」という意味。
  ここは、「ミルクをチーズへと変えていく工程を起動させる装置」という意味で、lactic starterは実際には乳酸菌への移行を促す工夫さすものと考えられる。
- □ are treated and pressed
  「(化学的に)処理されて圧力を加えられる」
- □ get hard and improve the flavor
  「固くなって風味を増す」

> ## 参考
>
> **チーズの定義(http://www.geocities.jp/cheeseforum/fdefinition.htm)**
> FAO[食糧農業機関]／WHO[世界保健機関]の定義によれば、チーズとは、フレッシュ又は熟成した、固形又は半固形の製品であり、下記のいずれかに基づき製造されたものをいいます。
> 1. レンネット(＝凝乳酵素)又はその他適当な凝固剤の作用により、乳, 脱脂乳、部分脱脂乳、クリーム、ホエークリーム、バターミルク又はこれらのどんな混合物であっても、それらを凝固させ、この凝固物より分離するホエーを部分的に流出せしめることで得られるもの。
> 2. 乳及び、または乳から得られる原料を用い、凝固を引き起こす加工技術により1に限定されている製品と同じ化学的、物理的、官能的な特徴をもつ最終的な製品。つまり、乳や、乳から得られる原料をもとに、自然に存在する乳酸菌と、酵素や凝固剤の作用によって、乳を凝固し、そこから乳清を取り除いたもの。分かり易く、チーズの製法を簡単に記すと、「(乳＋乳酸菌＋凝乳酵素)－乳清＝チーズ」となる。

Topic.51

What is a desert?

A desert is an area that receives 10 inches or less of precipitation (rain or snow) each year. Many of the world's deserts are found within 30 degrees latitude of the equator. You may have heard about hot deserts like the Sahara in northern Africa. The only precipitation hot deserts get is a little bit of rain. But there's another kind called a cold desert. The only precipitation cold deserts get is 10 or fewer inches of snow in a year. The Gobi Desert in China and Mongolia is a cold desert and so is the Great Basin Desert that stretches across Idaho, Nevada, Oregon, and Utah in the U.S.

専門用語

- ☐ precipitation　降水量
- ☐ hot desert　高温砂漠
- ☐ cold desert　寒冷地砂漠
- ☐ Mongolia　モンゴル

What is a desert? Topic. 51

[注]

- [ ] within 30 degrees latitude of the equator
  「赤道から南北の緯度が30度以内に」
- [ ] a little bit of rain　「ほんの少しばかりの雨」
- [ ] the Sahara　「サハラ砂漠」。アフリカ北部にある世界最大の砂漠。東西5600km、南北1700kmで面積は約1000万km²であり、アフリカ大陸の3分の1近くを占める。
- [ ] there's another kind called a cold desert
  「寒冷地砂漠と呼ばれている別種の砂漠がある」
- [ ] 10 or fewer inches　「10インチ以下」
- [ ] The Gobi Desert　「ゴビ砂漠」
- [ ] and so is the Great Basin Desert
  = and the Great Basin Desert is a cold desert, too.
  「グレートベイスン砂漠もまた寒冷地砂漠だ」
- [ ] stretches across Idaho, Nevada, Oregon, and Utah
  「アイダホ州、ネバダ州、オレゴン州、ユタ州にまたがって広がっている」

What is hypothermia? Topic.52

Hypothermia is when you have abnormally low body temperature, and it can happen if you fall into icy water or if you get lost in the snow for a long time. Signs of hypothermia include stumbling, shivering, irrational behavior, slurred speech, and pale, cold skin. Hypothermia is easy to prevent by protecting yourself from the cold and planning any cold-weather trips carefully with a knowledgeable adult. If you're out in the snow and suspect someone has hypothermia, stop what you're doing and get help immediately.

[専門用語]

- [ ] hypothermia　「低体温症」
- [ ] slur 〜　「〜を不明瞭に言う」

注

- abnormally low body temperature 「異常に低い体温」
- get lost in the snow 「雪の中で道に迷う」
- Signs of hypothermia 「低体温症の兆候」
- stumble 「よろめく」
- shiver 「震える」
- irrational behavior 「合理性を欠く振る舞い」
- slurred speech 「話が不明瞭であること」
- Hypothermia is easy to prevent
  = It is easy to prevent hypothermia 「低体温症を防ぐのは簡単だ」
- and (by) planning any cold-weather trips carefully with a knowledgeable adult
  「寒冷な気候の地域への旅行をするのなら、どんな旅行であっても知識の豊富な大人と一緒に注意深く計画を立てることによって」
- suspect (that) … 「…だろうと疑う」
- cf. doubt 「…ではないだろうと疑う」

Topic.53

How fast does a cat run?

A domestic cat like your own kitty can run up to 30mph. Most house cats don't run that fast unless they're scared by something. The fastest cat of all is the cheetah. These wild cats can run up to 70mph when they sprint after their prey. Cheetahs have long legs, a very flexible spine, and light bones that make them built for speed. They're the fastest animals on land!

専門用語

- cheetah チータ
- spine 背骨

注

- mph 「mile per hour」。(時速〜マイル)
- that fast 「そんなに早く」
- ※ thatは副詞で、「それほど」
- after their prey 「獲物を追いかけて」

What are the parts of the flower?　Topic.54

The four main parts of a flower are: petals, which have bright colors and come in all kinds of shapes; sepals, the small leaves underneath the flower; stamen, the long, dangly parts that produce pollen; and carpel, which receives pollen from the wind and insects inside the petal. Both the carpel and the stamen are reproductive organs. They also have smaller parts, much like the organs in your body.

専門用語
- petal　花弁　□ sepal　萼(がく)片
- stamen　雄しべ　□ dangly　ぶらさがった
- carpel　心皮(しんぴ。雌しべをつくりあげている構成要素)　しばしば pistil

注
- come in 「出現する」　□ pollen 「花粉」
- reproductive organ 「生殖器官」
- much like 〜 「〜とたいへんよく似て」

Why are the waves in Australia and Hawaii so big?　Topic.55

Big waves are formed by a number of different factors, but the main one is wind moving across water. Winds that blow strong and steadily for great distances will create large waves. Australia and Hawaii are exposed to these big winds, which are often called trade winds. They also have the right kinds of reefs and bays that are important in sculpting monster waves.

専門用語
- trade wind　貿易風

> 注
- □ for great distances 「長い距離にわたって」
- □ reef 「(さんご礁などの)礁」
- □ sculpt ＝ sculpture
  「～を彫刻で作る」。ここは彫刻の表面ででこぼこしているから、荒々しい海面をそれにたとえたもの

Topic.56

Who invented the compact disc?

A man named James T. Russell invented the compact disc in the late 1960s. Mr. Russell was a born inventor − when he was six he invented a remote controlled battleship that had a storage container for his lunch! He loved to listen to music, but was frustrated by the way old records and cassettes would wear out. So he invented a new recording system − one that would use light to read sounds. Today, this "digital to optical" recording technology is used in computers and stereos all around the world.

> 注
- □ remote controlled battleship
  「リモコンで動く戦艦」(もちろんおもちゃである)
- □ wear out 「すり減る」
- □ use light to read sounds
  「音を読み取るのに光を使う」。「光」というのは実際にはレーザーが使われている。

"digital to optical" recording technology

「『デジタルを光へ』方式の記録技術」。音波というアナログの信号を44,100分の1秒ごとのパルス信号に変え、これを0と1の組み合わせからなるデジタル信号に置き換える。次に、その0と1の符号をディスク上に突起が「ある・ない」で記録する。再生する場合、突起の「ある・ない」は光で読み取る。つまり、レーザー光を当てると、突起がなければ発射口の方に反射し、突起があれば左右に散乱してしまうような仕組みになっているわけだ。

What is the smallest ocean?

Topic.57

The Arctic Ocean is ten times smaller than the Pacific Ocean, and has about 1.5 times the surface area of the United States. It is the smallest of the four oceans, and is almost completely surrounded by land at the top of the globe. The middle of the Arctic Ocean is permanently covered by ten feet of ice! While many early scientists believed that no wildlife could exist in the Arctic Ocean, it is home to a bunch of animals, including polar bears.

注

- ☐ Arctic Ocean 「北極海」
- ☐ ten times smaller than the Pacific Ocean
  「太平洋の10倍の小ささだ→太平洋の10分の1の大きさだ」
- ☐ about 1.5 times the surface area of the United States
  「アメリカ合衆国の表面積のおよそ1.5倍の表面積」
- ☐ the four oceans 「4大洋」。ただし、通常は地理的に大海を5つに分割して、大西洋(Atlantic Ocean)、太平洋(Pacific Ocean)、インド洋(Indian Ocean)、北極海(Arctic Ocean)、南極海 (Antarctic Ocean)に区分している。
- ☐ at the top of the globe 「地球の一番上にあって」
- ☐ wildlife 「野生生物」
- ☐ is home to 「〜が存在する」
- ☐ a bunch of 〜 「〜の群れ」
- ☐ polar bear 「北極グマ」

What do tigers eat?

Topic.58

Tigers are at the top of the food chain, which means they eat anything they want! Tigers are predators, and have been known to eat crocodiles, birds, fish, reptiles, and even bears and leopards. Their favorite dinner, however, is often a hoofed animal like a deer or a pig. Their stripes not only look cool, but they also allow them to hide in tall grass. Some tigers can weigh up to seven hundred pounds!

[専門用語]
- [ ] reptile　爬虫類の動物　　[ ] leopard　　ヒョウ
- [ ] hoofed animal　有蹄動物（hoofは「ひづめ」）

[注]
- [ ] food chain　「食物連鎖」
- [ ] ,which means …　「それは次のことを意味する」
※ 関係代名詞whichの先行詞は直前の節の内容。
- [ ] predator　「捕食動物」（食物連鎖の上位にいる動物）
- [ ] look cool　「格好がよく見える」
- [ ] they allow them to hide in tall grass
「縞模様があるおかげで、トラは背の高い草の中にうまく隠れることができる」
- [ ] seven hundred pounds　「およそ318kg」

What are bones made of?

Topic.59

Your bones are very much alive. They are a mixture of hard, dense cells called calcium, and other cells that help them grow and mend themselves. Many bones are hollow and contain marrow, a soft material which makes the red and white cells in your blood. That's right, your bones help make your blood! It's important to keep your bones healthy by drinking lots of milk and eating your veggies. The human hand has 27 bones, and your face has 14!

[専門用語]
- [ ] hollow　中身の詰まっていない　　[ ] marrow　骨髄　　[ ] veggies　野菜

[注]
- [ ] very much alive　「とても活発で」。形容詞aliveは、叙述用法で用いることで有名だが、「活発な」という意味で使う場合には限定用法も可能。
- [ ] a mixture of hard, dense cells called calcium, and other cells that help them grow and mend themselves
「カルシウムと呼ばれる固くて密度の濃い細胞と、それらの細胞が成長したり自己修復するのを助ける役割を持った他の細胞から成り立っている」
- [ ] marrow, a soft material　「骨髄すなわち柔らかな物質」。同格表現である。
- [ ] red and white cells　「赤血球と白血球」
- [ ] help (to) make your blood　「血液を作る手助けをしている」

What is friction?

Topic.60

Friction is the force that occurs when any two objects come into contact with each other, like a wheel on a road or a runner sliding into third base. Friction slows down movement, and it's a very important element in designing things like brakes, highways, and even roller coasters.

専門用語
☐ brake　ブレーキ

注
☐ come into contact with 〜　「接触する」
☐ slide into 〜　「〜に滑りこむ」
☐ slow down　「速度を落とす」
☐ roller coaster　「ジェットコースター」

What is a lightning rod?

Topic.61

Lightning rods are long metal poles, usually found on top of tall buildings, that are intended to attract lightning and safely conduct it to the ground. They save buildings from being burned to the ground by lightning strikes. The lightning rod was invented by Benjamin Franklin, who was one of the first scientists to call lightning and electricity the same thing. Lightning is a very powerful form of negatively-charged electricity that naturally seeks out a positive charge on the ground. Tall objects like flagpoles and radio towers attract lightning.

専門用語
☐ lightning rod　避雷針　☐ flagpole　旗ざお

注
- that are intended to … 「…するように意図された」。関係代名詞thatの直前にカンマがあるが、これはこの関係代名詞が継続用法だということを示すものではない。限定用法である。usually found on top of tall buildingsの箇所を挿入するためのカンマ。
- attract lightning 「稲妻を引き寄せる」
- conduct it to the ground 「稲妻を地面へと導く」
- be burned to the ground 「焼け落ちる」
- lightning strikes 「稲妻の攻撃」
- call lightning and electricity the same thing 「稲妻と電気とは同じものだという」
- negatively-charged 「マイナス電気を帯びた」
- seeks out 〜 「〜を捜し求める」
- positive charge 「正の電荷」

Topic.62

How are coins made?

All coins start as long sheets of metal that are bound in coils and punched into disks by a machine called a blanking press. These disks are called blanks, and are scrubbed and cleaned before they become imprinted by a coining press. The coining press stamps the stuff you see on the coin, like the presidential profile and the amount. Then they're ready to jingle in your pocket!

専門用語
- jingle チリンチリンと鳴る

注
- sheets of metal 「薄板状の金属」
- are bound in coils 「ぐるぐる巻いて束ねられている」
- punch 〜 「〜(金属・皮・切符など)に穴をあける」
- disk 「円盤(状の物)」
- blanking press 圧穿機(あっせんき)。「(抜き型などで板金から〜…を)抜く機械」
- blank 「未完成金属片(ブランク)」
- cf. blanks for coins 「未刻片(貨幣刻印を押す前の金属片)」

How are coins made? **Topic 62**

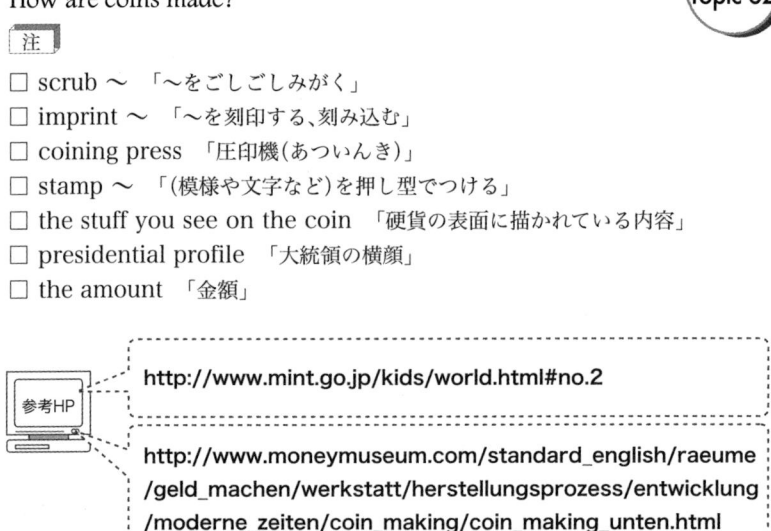

注

- [ ] scrub 〜 「〜をごしごしみがく」
- [ ] imprint 〜 「〜を刻印する、刻み込む」
- [ ] coining press 「圧印機(あついんき)」
- [ ] stamp 〜 「(模様や文字など)を押し型でつける」
- [ ] the stuff you see on the coin 「硬貨の表面に描かれている内容」
- [ ] presidential profile 「大統領の横顔」
- [ ] the amount 「金額」

参考HP

http://www.mint.go.jp/kids/world.html#no.2

http://www.moneymuseum.com/standard_english/raeume/geld_machen/werkstatt/herstellungsprozess/entwicklung/moderne_zeiten/coin_making/coin_making_unten.html

What is censorship? **Topic.63**

Censorship is the act of banning speech or writing, often by governments who judge it to be somehow bad or immoral. It's an ugly practice that has a very long and sad history. Many books are banned because they are critical of the government, or they have material that someone finds immoral or offensive. In the U.S., several important works of literature like "Huckleberry Finn" by Mark Twain and "Ulysses" by James Joyce were once banned. Some people have even tried to ban the Harry Potter books.

専門用語

- [ ] censorship 検閲

注

- ban speech or writing 「スピーチや執筆を禁止する」
- judge it to be somehow bad or immoral
「そのスピーチや執筆がどういうわけか悪いか道徳に反していると判断する」。
cf. judge 〜 to be … 「〜が…だと判断する」
- be critical of 〜 「〜を厳しく批判している」
- material 「題材」
- works of literature 「文学作品」
- Mark Twain 「マーク・トウェイン」。アメリカの作家(1835-1910)。
「トム・ソーヤの冒険」、「ハックルベリー・フィンの冒険」などが特に有名。
- James Joyce 「ジェイムズ・ジョイス」。アイルランドの小説家(1882-1941)。
「ユリシーズ」、「ダブリン市民」などが特に有名。
- Harry Potter J.K.ローリング(J.K.Rowling)作のHarry Potterシリーズ物をさす。

Topic.64

How do clowns fit in their small car?

The clown car trick is a circus classic that involves lots of clowns pouring out of a tiny car. I couldn't find a concrete answer to your question, but I'd say the clown car trick is an illusion, a trick that involves not showing the audience the whole story. Since the clowns can't all fit in the car, I'd guess there are a bunch of clowns hiding under a trapdoor in the floor beneath the car, who then climb out of the car like they've been in there all along.

専門用語
- clown (サーカスの)道化師

注
- clown car trick 「(サーカスで)道化師が小さな車から続々と出てくるマジック」
- circus classic 「伝統的なサーカスの出し物」
- pour out of 〜 「〜から続々と出てくる」
- concrete answer to your question 「あなたの質問に対する具体的な答」

Topic 64

How do clowns fit in their small car?

注

- □ illusion 「錯覚」
- □ a trick that involves not showing 〜
  「〜を示さないことを必然的結果として伴うトリック」
- cf. involve …ing 「…することを(必然的結果として)伴う」
- → involve not …ing 「…しないことを(必然的結果として)伴う」
- ※ なお、an illusionと直後のa trickとは同格。
- □ show the audience the whole story 「観客に一部始終(事の顛末)を示す」
- □ all fit in the car 「全員が車の中にはまる」
- □ a bunch of 〜 「〜の群れ」
- □ trapdoor 「(舞台の)上げぶた」
- □ climb out of the car 「手足を使ってはうように車から出てくる」。climbという動詞は必ずしも、「上に進む」ことを意味しない。「(手足を使ってはうように)進む」
- □ like they've been in there all along
  「彼らはまるでずっとそこに(車の中に)いたかのように」
- ※ 接続詞のlike(あたかも…のように)は、as if …のような意味を持つが、as ifと異なり、通常は直説法の英文が続く。(仮定法の英文を続けない)
- □ all along 「最初からずっと」

Topic 65

What's the story behind potato chips?

Fried potatoes were brought to the United States by Thomas Jefferson in the late 18th century (he found them in France, though they're originally from Belgium), but the potato chip as we know it today was invented in 1853 in a diner in New York state called Moon's Lake House. As the story goes, a surly cook named George Crum, angry at a customer's complaint that his potatoes weren't fried enough, chopped several potatoes into paper-thin slices and fried them. The new "Saratoga Chips" proved a hit, and potato chips were in thousands of grocery stores by the end of the 19th century.

専門用語
- surly　ぶっきらぼうな

注
- Thomas Jefferson
  「トマス・ジェファーソン」。米国第3代大統領(在任1801-09)。
- the potato chip as we know it today
  「今日私たちが知っているようなポテトチップス」
- a diner in New York state　「ニューヨーク州にある簡易食堂」
- as the story goes　「その話によると」
  ＝ according to the story
- angry at a customer's complaint　「客の不平に腹を立てて」
※ beingが省略された分詞構文。
- complaint that his potatoes weren't fried enough
  「ポテトが十分に揚げられていないという(内容の)不平」
※ thatは同格節を導く接続詞。
- chopped several potatoes into paper-thin slices
  「数個のポテトを切り刻んで紙のように薄いスライスにした」
※ a surly cookが主語でchoppedはその述語動詞。
- Saratoga Chips　「サラトガチップス」
  本文に出てくるa diner in New York stateはニューヨーク州のSaratoga Springsにあったのでこのような名前をつけたのであろう。
- proved a hit　「ヒット商品となった」
cf. prove (to be) ～　「～となる、～であることが判明する」

How long does it take for a dog to have puppies?

Topic.66

The time during which a mother is pregnant with a baby is called the gestation period. The average gestation period for dogs is quite short – about sixty days. Humans, for instance, have a gestation period of about nine months, while for elephants it's almost two years! Did you know that the largest litter ever recorded was twenty-three puppies?

How　　　　　　　　　　　　　　　　　　　　Topic 66

専門用語
□ pregnant　妊娠している　□ gestation period　妊娠期間
□ litter　（ブタ・イヌなどの）一腹の子
　(five puppies at a litter　「一腹の５匹の子イヌ」)

注
□ while　「その一方で」。接続詞

What are windmills?

Topic.67

　Windmills are machines that people use to grind grain, pump water, and create electricity. They were first invented around 600 A.D., and early windmills looked like merry-go-rounds with vertical blades. They were used to grind grain into flour. In the 1100s, windmills with blades or sails that turned on a horizontal shaft became popular. These were more powerful windmills, and the Dutch people used them to pump water to where they wanted it. In the 1970s, people started using high-tech windmills called turbines to harness wind power. The energy captured by wind turbines can power cities, so windmills are still a part of our lives and may help us more in the future.

専門用語
□ vertical　垂直な　□ blade　回転翼の羽根
□ horizontal shaft　水平な軸
□ high-tech　ハイテク技術を使った
□ turbine　タービン

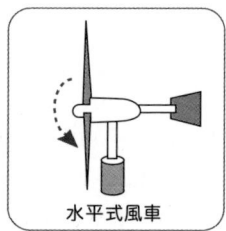

垂直式風車　　　水平式風車

注

- [ ] grind grain, pump water, and create electricity
  「穀物を挽いたり、水を汲み上げたり、電気を創ったりする」
- [ ] windmills with blades or sails that turned on a horizontal shaft
  「水平な軸にくっついた(=on)羽根が回転する風車」。現在、日本の各地で見られる大型の風車の形である。家庭用の扇風機によく似た形を想像するとよい。sailは、羽根の一種。昔は羽根の部分を金属などで作らないで、帆船の帆に使うような頑丈な布を使っていた地域もあった。
- [ ] to (the place) where they wanted it
  「その水を必要とするところへ」
  ※ 関係副詞whereは先行詞が the placeの場合、この先行詞を省略することがある。
- [ ] harness wind power　「風力を作りだす」
- [ ] power cities　「町に電力を供給する」

Topic.68

Where does sand come from?

Sand comes from rocks – in fact, sand is just ground up rock! Wind, water, and other movement can break down rocks over time until sand grains are formed. Different types of sand are created from different rocks. Black-sand beaches in Hawaii are made up of volcanic rock and glass. The yellow sandy beaches of southern California are made of quartz and other minerals that are found in the nearby mountains. Sometimes sand is made of organic materials that are worn down into bits. Shells, coral, and the skeletons of tiny sea creatures can all become sand.

専門用語

- [ ] volcanic rock　火山岩
- [ ] volcanic glass　火山玻璃 (はりとは「水晶」のこと)
- [ ] coral　サンゴ

Where does sand come from?　Topic 68

|注|

☐ Sand comes from rocks　「砂の元は岩である」
☐ just ground up rock　「細かく砕かれた岩にすぎない」
※ groundはgrindの過去分詞形で、「砕かれた」。up は副詞で、「すっかり」。
☐ break down　「破壊する」
☐ over time　「長い間に」
☐ sand grain　「砂の粒」
☐ be made (up) of ～　「～でできている」
☐ quartz　「石英」
☐ organic materials　「有機物質」
☐ are worn down into bits　「摩滅して小片になる」
cf. wear down ～　「摩滅させる、すり減らす」
☐ skeletons of tiny sea creatures　「小さな海の生き物たちの残骸（ざんがい）」

参考HP　http://www.volcanogallery.com/Places-Punaluu.htm

How do you change between Celsius and Fahrenheit?　Topic.69

To go from Celsius to Fahrenheit, multiply the temperature number by 9, then divide by 5, and add 32. To go from Fahrenheit to Celsius, subtract 32 from the temperature number, then multiply by 5, and divide by 9.

|専門用語|
☐ Celsius　摂氏　☐ Fahrenheit　華氏

|注|
要するに本文の内容を公式に直せば次の通り。たとえば、9をかけて5で割るということは、1.8をかけるということに等しい。

> ●摂氏から華氏への変換　　$F = 1.8C + 32$
>
> ●華氏から摂氏への変換　　$C = \dfrac{5}{9}(F-32)$

Topic.70

What is a fossil?

A German physician in 1546 first used the term "fossils" to describe many types of minerals, stones, and archeological items. The word comes from the Latin word for "something dug up." Today only things that give evidence of a formerly living creature are fossils. Bones, teeth, eggs, scales, and shells of an animal can be fossils, and so can footprints and teeth marks. Fossilized insects have been found in amber, which is hardened tree sap. Plants can leave fossil traces too, like when a leaf shape is imprinted into stone.

専門用語

☐ footprint　足跡
☐ fossilize ～　～を化石化する
☐ amber　琥珀(こはく。地中に埋没した樹脂が化石化したもの。)
☐ sap　樹液

注

☐ something dug up　「掘り当てられたもの」
※ dig - dug - dug
☐ and so can footprints and teeth marks.
　＝ and footprints and teeth marks can be fossils, too.
　「それから足跡や歯型も化石になりうる」
☐ teeth mark　「歯型」

Why is Mars red?

Mars is red because it's rusting! The red color of the planet comes from the oxidation of iron minerals in the soil. The rusty dirt is blown all over the planet by strong winds. But scientists think there isn't much iron inside Mars. The planet is only 75% as dense as the Earth and doesn't have a strong magnetic field like the Earth does. So Mars probably doesn't have a nickel/iron core inside. Mars only has a lot of rusty iron oxide on the surface. Did you know Mars' name comes from its red color? The ancient Romans named the planet Mars after their god of war because the planet looked blood stained!

[専門用語]
- ☐ rust　(鉄などが)さびる　☐ oxidation　酸化　☐ iron oxide　酸化鉄

[注]
- ☐ because it's rusting!　「さびているからだ」。動詞rustには、「さびる」が転じて、「(才能などが使わないために)だめになる」という意味もある。
  ここは、火星は、「地球と違って人のような生物が住んでいないからだめになっている星」というニュアンスも含むように思われる。
- ☐ rusty dirt is blown all over the planet
  「さびたほこりが火星中に吹き飛ばされる」
- ☐ 75% as dense as the Earth　「地球の密度の75%の密度」
- ☐ magnetic field　「磁場」
- ☐ nickel/iron core　「ニッケルや鉄でできたコア」。コアは中心核とも言う。
  外核の半径は3500km、内核の半径は1250kmである。
  なお、地球の平均密度は5515kg/㎥であり、太陽系で最も密度の高い惑星である。
  表面付近の密度は3000 kg/㎥程度であり、核は非常に高密度な状態である。
  ほとんどは鉄 (80%) とニッケルから成る。
- ☐ ancient Romans　「古代ローマ人」
- ☐ <u>named</u> <u>the planet</u> <u>Mars</u>　「その惑星をMarsと名づけた」
  　(V)　　(O)　　　(C)
- ☐ after their god of war　「戦いの神(の名に)ちなんで」
- ☐ blood stained　「血で汚れた」

Topic.72

Do whales have teeth?

Some do and some don't! Whales are classified into two main groups. The first are toothed whales of the suborder *Odontoceti*, which have lots of teeth that they use to catch fish and other sea animals. This group includes killer whales, sperm whales, and also dolphins and porpoises (which are whales too). The second type are baleen whales of the suborder *Mysticeti*, and instead of teeth, they have plates in their mouths that act like giant filters to strain tiny sea creatures out of the water. Humpback whales and grey whales are baleen whales. In fact, the biggest animal that ever existed − even bigger than the dinosaurs − is the blue whale, and it doesn't have any teeth!

|専門用語|

- ☐ suborder *Odontoceti*　ハクジラ亜目　☐ killer whale　シャチ
- ☐ sperm whale　マッコウクジラ
- ☐ porpoise　ネズミイルカ
- ☐ suborder *Mysticeti*　ヒゲクジラ亜目
- ☐ humpback whale　ザトウクジラ
- ☐ grey whale　コククジラ
- ☐ blue whale　シロナガスクジラ

|注|

- ☐ are classified into 〜　「〜に分類される」
- ☐ strain tiny sea creatures out of the water
  「水から小さな海の生物を漉(こ)す」

参考HP　http://www.gem.hi-ho.ne.jp/aquaheart/whaledictionary.html

What is a blizzard? Topic.73

Blizzards are giant snow storms that disrupt people's lives and cause a lot of damage. There are a lot of ways to measure the severity of winter storms: the amount of snow that falls in a given amount of time, the speed of the wind, and the distance that you can see. A blizzard is defined as a snow storm that has winds blowing over 35 miles an hour, and a visibility (or the distance you can see) of less than 400 meters. These conditions have to last for at least three hours for the storm to be called a blizzard. If you live in an area that has a lot of heavy snow, you should take some precautions, or actions that will help your safety.

専門用語
- blizzard　ブリザード

注
- disrupt people's lives 「人々の暮らしを混乱させる」
- severity 「激しさ」＜ severe 「厳しい」
- last for at least three hours 「少なくとも3時間続く」
- for the storm to be called a blizzard
「嵐がブリザードと呼ばれるためには」。不定詞の前に、「不定詞の意味上の主語」が付いている形。
- take precautions 「用心をする、警戒する」

How does your stomach work? Topic.74

The stomach is part of the digestive system, which has all the parts of your body that eat food, get nutrients from it, and pass the waste out. After you chew and swallow your food, it travels through a tube called the esophagus into your stomach. This is where the food gets churned and mashed into a liquid mixture. On the outside, your stomach has strong muscles to mash food. Inside, it's full of acids and gastric juices that break food down into bits. Food spends two to four hours inside your stomach, until it's mushy enough to go into your intestines. That's where nutrients are removed from the food.

|専門用語|
- ☐ esophagus　食道　☐ churn　かき混ぜる　☐ mash　押しつぶす
- ☐ gastric juices　胃液　☐ mushy　柔らかな　☐ intestines　腸(通常複数形)

|注|
- ☐ digestive system　「消化器系」
- ☐ get nutrients　「栄養を取り入れる」
- ☐ pass the waste out　「廃棄物を排泄する」
- ☐ chew and swallow your food　「食べ物を(歯で)かんで飲み込む」
- ☐ This is where …　「これは…する場所だ」。関係副詞whereの先行詞が the place の場合、省略されることも多い。
- ☐ This is where the food gets churned and mashed into a liquid mixture. 「ここは食べ物がかき混ぜられ、押しつぶされて液体(胃液)と混ざり合うところだ」
- ☐ on the outside　「(胃袋の)外側は」
- ☐ mash ～　「～を押しつぶす」
- ☐ acids and gastric juices　「酸と胃液」
- ☐ break food down　「食べ物を分解する」
- ☐ two to four hours　「2時間から4時間」

How long can a person live without water?

Topic.75

It depends on how hot it is, but an average person would be very lucky to survive eight to ten days without water. Water is incredibly important to the human body. If you were on a desert island, and someone offered you a bunch of food or a bunch of water, you should definitely go with the water. Your body is over 50% water, and you should drink at least two or three big cups of it a day. Water helps regulate your body temperature, carries energy, and helps expel waste. Don't leave home without it!

How long can a person live without water? Topic 75

専門用語
- desert island　無人島

注
- It depends on how hot it is　「暑さ次第だ」

cf. depend on ～　「～次第だ」。ここは名詞節が前置詞onの目的語になっている。

- to survive eight to ten days without water
  「もしも水なしで8日から10日の間生き延びることができたら」。仮定法で、不定詞の箇所がIf節の代わりをしている例。
- definitely　「確実に」
- go with ～　「～を選ぶ」
- regulate your body temperature　「あなたの体温を調整する」
- expel waste　「老廃物を追い出す」

What is puberty? Topic.76

Puberty is when your body starts changing from being a kid's body to an adult's body. Lots of different things can happen: your voice might start making all kinds of strange noises, hairs start sprouting in all sorts of places, you want to sleep a lot, your clothes don't fit all of a sudden — it can be strange! It usually happens to girls a couple of years before it happens to boys, which can make things even weirder. There are often emotional changes, too, so you might be particularly grouchy, or find that you get upset more easily. It helps to remember that the stuff you're going through is normal, and everyone's dealing with it.

専門用語
- puberty　思春期　　□ sprout　生え始める
- grouchy　不機嫌な

注

- [ ] making all kinds of strange noises
 「今まで経験したこともないようなあらゆる種類の音を出す」
- [ ] all of a sudden 「突然に」＝ suddenly
- [ ] a couple of years before … 「…する2、3年前に」
※ このbeforeは接続詞。a couple of years（2、3年）は副詞句として接続詞を修飾している。
- [ ] even weirder 「ずいぶんと変な」
※ evenは比較級を強調する役割を果たしている。
- [ ] It helps to remember that the stuff you're going through is normal
 「あなたが経験していることは普通のことなのだということを覚えておくと役に立つよ」
※ Itはto remember 以下を表す仮主語。helpはここでは自動詞で、「役に立つ」。
※ go through 〜＝ experience 〜
- [ ] deal with 〜 「〜（問題など）を処理する」

Why does your nose run when you cry?

Topic.77

Great observation! I've noticed that as well. As it turns out, your nose runs for the same reason your eyes water. Crying is part of our body's reaction to pain, and is supposed to flush out bad stuff from our eyes. When your nose runs, your body is also trying to flush out potentially harmful matter from your mucous membranes. Your mucous membranes are the moist, sensitive parts of your body that are in contact with the air, like your eyes and the inner lining of your nose.

専門用語

- [ ] mucous membrane　粘膜

注

- [ ] as well 「…もまた」
- [ ] as it turns out 「結局のところ」
- [ ] the same reason your eyes water
 「あなたの目が涙を流すのと同じ理由」。reasonの後ろに関係副詞whyが省略されている。

Why does your nose run when you cry? Topic 77

注

□ and (crying) is supposed to flush out bad stuff from our eyes
「涙を流すということは、私たちの目から悪いもの(異物)を流しだすよう意図されていることだ」
cf. be supposed to …　「…するよう意図されている、…するはずだ」
※ flush out　「どっと流し出す」
□ potentially harmful matter　「(やがては)害になりそうなもの」
□ like your eyes and the inner lining of your nose
→ これは前の文全体にかかっている。「目や鼻の内側の層と同じように(空気と接触している湿っていて敏感な部位だ)」
□inner lining of your nose　「鼻の内側の層」

How was Jupiter formed? Topic.78

Jupiter is the biggest planet in our solar system – it's 318 times the size of the Earth! Since it's so big, it was named after the Roman king of the gods. You could almost fly right through Jupiter in a space ship. It's made up of very dense gas, but has a solid core about the size of Earth. Like the other planets in our solar system, Jupiter was formed about 4.5 billion years ago when a giant blob of gas and dust started collapsing together. Unlike planets like Mars and Earth, this cloud of cosmic dust was never dense enough to form a solid sphere.

専門用語

□ blob　ぼんやりとしたもの

注

□ solar system　「太陽系」
□ 318 times the size of the Earth　「地球の大きさの318倍」
□ You could almost fly right through Jupiter in a space ship.
「もしかしたら宇宙船で木星を通り抜けることだってできるかもしれない」
※ couldは仮定法を表すための助動詞として使われている。
※ fly right through ～　「～を飛行して通りぬける」

cf. fly through the clouds(雲間を飛行する)。sleep right through the earthquake(地震の間中ずっと眠っている)。なお、almost(ほとんど)がある理由は、後ろの文に書かれている通り、木星はガスだけでできているのではなくて、中心部には地球大の核が存在するからである。
- is made up of 〜　「〜から成り立っている」
- a solid core about the size of Earth　「地球とほぼ同じ大きさの固い核」
- collapse　「(膨張していたものが)しぼむ」。ここでは、「崩壊する」ではない。輪郭のはっきりしない巨大なガスが現在の木星のような形へとまとまり始めたことをさしている。
- was never dense enough to form a solid sphere
「固体の球を形作るほど密度が濃くならなかった」

Why do roses have thorns?

Topic.79

Roses have thorns to protect them. Thorns ward off potential nibblers – grazing animals like goats or cows who might eat rose plants for food. One mouth full of thorns, and they look elsewhere for dinner! Many plants have protective mechanisms like spines, thorns, and poison to ward off hungry herbivores. A herbivore is an animal that eats only plants.

専門用語
- thorn　とげ　　ward off　寄せつけない
- nibbler　かじるもの
- grazing animal　草食動物　　spines　(サボテンなどの)とげ
- herbivore　草食動物

注
- might eat rose plants for food
「ひょっとしたら食事用にバラの木を食べるかもしれない」
- One mouth full of thorns, and they look elsewhere for dinner!
「口の中がとげだらけになれば、食事としてはどこか他をさがすことになる」。
※"命令文, and …"　(〜しなさい。そうすれば…だ)の構文に近いニュアンスを持つ。とげのあるバラの木をかじってみると、痛いのでそれに懲りて(食事用には)他をさがすという意味。

Topic.80

What is the smallest country?

The smallest official country in the world is Vatican City, which is located inside Rome, Italy. While this country is only 0.2 square miles in area, it is a very important place for the billion practicing Catholics on Earth. Vatican City is the seat of the Catholic Church, and is where the Pope resides. Up until the late 19th century, the popes used to rule Italy. Democratic reforms led to the establishment of the Vatican City in 1929 as a separate country.

専門用語

- □ Vatican City　バチカン市国(ユネスコの世界遺産)
- □ the Pope　ローマ教皇

注

- □ square miles in area　「～平方マイルの面積」。0.44km²。
- □ practicing Catholic　「実践的なカトリック教徒」
- □ seat of ～　「～の所在地」
- □ where the Pope resides　「ローマ教皇が住んでいる場所」
※ 先行詞のthe placeは省略されている。
- □ up until ～　「～まで」≒ until ～
- □ the popes used to rule Italy　「教皇たちがイタリアを統治していた」。全イタリアを継続的に統治していたという意味ではないので注意。イタリアは外部からの侵入が繰り返されるなど複雑な歴史を持っている。その複雑な歴史の中で教皇が統治する時代もあったという意味である。

参考HP　http://www.abacci.com/atlas/history.asp?countryID=229

- □ democratic reforms　「民主改革」
- □ lead to ～　「～を引き起こす」
cf. bring about ～
- □ as a separate country　「別個の国として」

What is diabetes?

Topic.81

People who have diabetes are not able to produce insulin, which is important in digesting sugar. As a result, they tend to have high sugar levels in their blood, which is bad for the body. There are two kinds of diabetes – the first kind is hereditary, and the second kind (90% of all cases) can be controlled by diet. Millions of people have diabetes and lead very happy, productive lives by monitoring their blood sugar levels.

専門用語
- diabetes　糖尿病　☐ insulin　インシュリン

注
- digest sugars　「糖を消化する」
- have high sugar levels in their blood　「(血液中の)血糖値が高い」
- lead very happy, productive lives　「とても幸せで生産的な生活を送る」
- monitor their blood sugar levels　「血糖値をチェックする」

参考

血糖値とは、血液内のブドウ糖(glucose)の濃度のこと。
血糖値は膵臓より分泌されるインシュリンによりそのレベルが維持されている。インシュリンの分泌量が減ったり、作用が弱くなると、血糖値は高い値を示すようになる。食後二時間血糖値でおおよそ180mg/dl～200mg/dl以上を示す状態を糖尿病と呼ぶ。

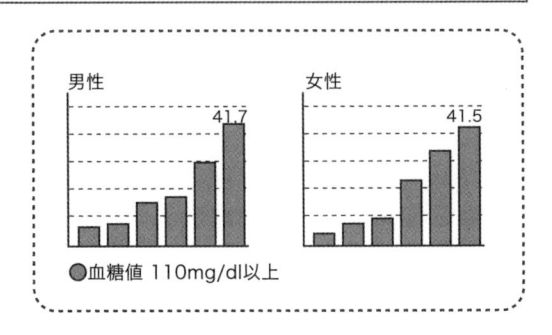

男性　　　　　　　　　女性
　　　　　41.7　　　　　　　　41.5

●血糖値 110mg/dl以上

Are dolphins mammals?

Dolphins are mammals, just like you and I are! All mammals are warm-blooded and hairy (instead of scaly), and the females give birth to live babies and produce milk for them. Unlike fish, dolphins need to breathe air. Fish get oxygen underwater through their gills, but dolphins don't have gills. Instead, dolphins rise to the water's surface to inhale and exhale. They have blowholes that are like nostrils, and strong muscles open and close the blowhole at the right time so the dolphins can breathe. Another way to tell a dolphin from a fish is by the shape of the tail. A fish's tail is vertical on its body, and the tail moves from side to side. A dolphin's tail is horizontal and moves up and down.

|専門用語|

- □ scaly　うろこのある　　□ gill　えら
- □ blowhole　（クジラ類の)噴水孔
- □ nostril　鼻の穴

|注|

- □ give birth to 〜　「〜を産む」
- □ inhale and exhale = breathe　「呼吸する」
- □ inhale　「(空気・ガスなど)を吸い込む」
- ※ exhale　「(息など)を吐き出す」
- □ so (that) the dolphins can breathe
　「イルカが呼吸をすることができるように」
- cf. so that S can … (…することができるように)の構文は、口語表現ではthatが省略されることも多い。
- □ tell a dolphin from a fish　「イルカと魚とを区別する」
- cf. tell A from B　「AとBとを区別する」
- □ vertical　「垂直の、直立した」
- □ horizontal　「水平な、横の」

Topic.83
Will sugar make water boil faster?

No, because a sugar solution has a higher boiling point than water (which means that it boils at a higher temperature). The greater the concentration of sugar in the water, the higher the boiling point. Dissolving chemicals in water generally raises its boiling point, because it becomes denser, or has more mass in the same amount of volume.

専門用語
- mass　粒子などの集積

注
- sugar solution
「砂糖水」。正式には、溶質である砂糖を、溶媒である水に溶かしたもの。
- boiling point　「沸点」。ある液体が沸騰を開始する温度。
- The greater the concentration of sugar in the water, the higher the boiling point.
「水の中の砂糖の濃度が高ければ高いほど、沸点は高くなる」

cf. the 比較級〜、the 比較級…の構文　「〜すればするほど…だ」

※ concentration of sugar　「砂糖の濃度」
- dissolving chemicals　「溶けている化学物質(本文の例では砂糖をさす)」

※ dissolve　「〜を溶かす、溶ける」
- amount of volume　「体積」

参考【沸点上昇】　不揮発性の物質(本文では砂糖)を一定量の溶媒(本文では水)に溶かした希薄溶液(本文では砂糖水)の蒸気圧は、純溶媒(水)のそれより低下するため、溶液(砂糖水)の沸点は純溶媒(水)の沸点より高くなる。この現象を沸点上昇という。

純粋液体の一定圧力下での沸点はその液体に固有の値となるが、圧力が異なると沸点は変化する。たとえば水の1気圧での沸点は100℃であるが、高地などの気圧が低いところでは水は100℃より低い温度で沸騰する。また、液体に物質が溶けていると蒸気圧降下に伴って沸点は上昇する(沸点上昇)。
(http://ja.wikipedia.org/wiki/%E8%92%B8%E6%B0%97%E5%9C%A7%E9%99%8D%E4%B8%8B)
富士山での炊飯実験:炊飯ジャーでは米が煮えきらない。
上空7000メートルでのお湯沸かし実験:0.4気圧では, 水の沸騰点は77度だった(富士山では88度)。加圧タンク内でのお湯沸かし実験:圧力鍋と同じ2気圧では, 水の沸騰点は120度だった。
(http://www.nhk.or.jp/gatten/archive/1999q4/19991006.html)

How many satellites are there around the Earth?

Topic.84

A satellite is any object that orbits a larger object. The Moon is the biggest satellite of the Earth, and there are many smaller satellites made and launched by people. An astronomer says that there are currently 2,671 satellites orbiting the Earth. That doesn't count space probes and space garbage (which includes some old satellites) — if you added those in, you'd have about 9,000 satellites! Countries launch satellites to help with communications, predict weather, provide global positioning services, study the Earth's surface, and perform scientific research.

専門用語
- space probes and space garbage　宇宙探査機や宇宙のゴミ

注
- global positioning services Global Positioning System services
「全地球測位システム(人工衛星などからの電波によって自分の位置を確かめる装置)を使ったサービス」。GPSサービス。

How far away are stars? What's the closest one?

Topic.85

The closest star to the Earth is the Sun! On average, the Sun is only 93 million miles away. Bigger distances in space are measured in light years, and one light year is about 6,000,000,000,000 miles. Aside from the Sun, Proxima Centauri is the closest star at 4.2 light years away. Some of the brightest stars are more distant — Rigel, in the constellation Orion, is the seventh brightest star in the sky but is 900 light years away. To see the most distant stars, astronomers use the Hubble Space Telescope. Hubble has seen galaxies full of stars that are 12 billion light years away!

|専門用語|
- □ light year　光年　□ Proxima Centauri　プロキシマケンタウリ星
- □ Rigel　リゲル　□ constellation Orion　オリオン座

|注|
- □ Aside from the Sun　「太陽を別とすれば」
- cf. aside from ～　「～を別にして」
- □ Hubble Space Telescope
   「ハッブル宇宙望遠鏡(アメリカが大気の影響を受けずに観測できるように、周回軌道に打ち上げた光学望遠鏡)」
- □ 12 billion light years　「120億光年」

Topic.86
Who invented baseball?

　Baseball doesn't have one single inventor, and if someone tells you that a man named Abner Doubleday invented baseball, feel free to tell them that they are full of horsefeathers! People have been hitting balls with sticks and running between bases for hundreds of years. The game we now know as baseball is a mix of very old games called "base" or "rounders." The basic rules of modern baseball were made official in 1845 by several amateur teams playing in New York.

|専門用語|
- □ horsefeathers　(米俗)(単数・複数扱い)たわごと
- □ rounders　ラウンダーズ(野球に似た球技)

|注|
- □ feel free to …　「遠慮なく…する」
- □ tell them that…　「その人たちに…だと言う」。someoneをtheyで受けているのは、そのようなこと(著者に言わせると「たわごと」)を言う人は何人もいると考えられるから。
- □ they are full of horsefeathers!　このtheyは、野球の起源に関する様々な話。
- □ The game we now know as baseball
   「私たちが今日野球として知っているゲーム」
- □ were made official　「公式化した」

Who invented baseball?　　　　Topic.86

Abner Doubledayに関しては、次のサイトが参考になる。
http://www.tulane.edu/~latner/Doubleday.html

How does a battery work?　Topic.87

A battery is basically a container of chemicals that creates electrons. When you put a battery in a radio, these electrons rush from the negative terminal of the battery to the positive terminal, powering the radio. Electricity is simply the movement of electrons through a conductive material like a copper wire. An Italian man named Alessandro Volta made the first battery in 1800. He discovered that different types of metals, when placed next to each other in salt water, create an electrochemical reaction which creates a current of electrons.

専門用語
- electron　電子
- Alessandro Volta　アレッサンドロ・ボルタ(1745-1827)
- electrochemical reaction　電気化学反応

注
- container of chemicals　「(複数種類の)化学物質を入れたもの」
- put a battery in a radio　「ラジオに電池をセットする」
- rush from the negative terminal of the battery to the positive terminal
  「電池の負極から正極へと突進していく」
- powering the radio　「ラジオに動力を供給して」。この文は分詞構文。
- through a conductive material like a copper wire
  「たとえば銅線のような導電体を通って」
- ※ conductive material　「導電体(一般に電気を流すもの)」。電気を流さないものは insulating material(絶縁体)。
- cf. semiconductor material　「半導体」

☐ when (they are) placed next to each other in salt water
「２種類の金属が塩水の中でお互いに隣同士に置かれると」
☐ current of electrons 「電子の流れ」

> 参考
>
> **ボルタの電池**　Alessandro Voltaが発明した世界最初の電池。２種類の金属（例えば銅と亜鉛）を電解液中に浸すと、２つの金属の酸化電位差から、亜鉛が酸化され電子を放出し、外部回路に電流が流れる。

参考HP: http://www.kahaku.go.jp/special/past/italia/ipix/b3f/2/5.html

Topic.88

How did the Earth form?

The Earth is about four and a half billion years old. Like all planets, the Earth began as a huge cloud of dust and gas that was thrown off by the sun. This huge cloud eventually gathered into a dense ball of matter. How does this happen? As the clump of space dust grows bigger, it gathers more gravity, pulling more matter in and eventually forming a semi-solid ball like the Earth. This process involves a lot of energy and heat. The temperatures at the center of the Earth are hotter than the surface of the Sun!

|専門用語|
☐ clump　かたまり　☐ semi-solid　半固体の

|注|
☐ four and a half billion years old 「45億年」
※ a half billion years ＝ 0.5×10億年で、「５億年」
☐ throw off 〜　「(熱や光を)放つ、産む、出す」
☐ involve 〜　「(結果として必然的に)〜を伴う」

Why is the sun yellow and not green?

Topic.89

Our sun is a star, and all stars emit different colors of light depending on their temperature. The coolest stars glow deep red, warmer ones glow yellow, and very hot stars glow blue. Have you ever noticed how a gas grill glows yellow at the bottom, then blue at the top? The blue part of the flame is much hotter.

注

☐ how a gas grill glows yellow at the bottom, then blue at the top
「ガス・グリル(の炎)が下の方では黄色い光を放ち、最上部あたりでは青い光を放っている様子」

☆星の色	☆青白	☆白	☆黄白	☆黄	☆橙	☆赤
表面温度	1万以上	1万~7000	7000~6000	6000	6000~3500	3500以下

What is a fairy tale?

Topic.90

Fairy tales are usually short stories that may include magical creatures or actions. Many fairy tales have been told and retold for hundreds of generations and weren't written down until recently. Some fairy tales have a moral or message that you are supposed to learn from, but the stories are for entertainment too. Different cultures sometimes have the same fairy tales that are only different in the details. For example, China, Italy, Germany, and many other countries all have versions of the Cinderella fairy tale.

注

☐ write down 「書きとめる」
☐ moral or message that you are supposed to learn from
「あなたが学ぶべき教訓やことづて」

cf. be supposed to … 「…することになっている、…すべきだ、…するよう意図されている、…するはずだ」
☐ Different cultures sometimes have the same fairy tales that are only different in the details.
「異なった文化圏に、細部だけ異なる同じような内容のお伽話が存在することがある」
☐ versions of the Cinderella fairy tale 「シンデレラ物語の変形版」

Topic.91

What is celluloid exactly?

Celluloid was the first synthetic plastic material, and it was invented in 1869. It was used in all kinds of household items, from toys to hair combs, for many years. But celluloid has one big problem – it can catch fire easily. Early in the 20th century, nonflammable plastics were created that replaced celluloid in many items. But it's still used to make film, both for cameras and for movies. That's why people sometimes refer to celluloid when they talk about the movies!

専門用語
☐ celluloid　セルロイド　☐ nonflammable　不燃性の

注
☐ synthetic plastic material　「合成のプラスチック材料」
☐ household item　「家財道具」
☐ catch fire easily　「燃えやすい」
☐ nonflammable plastics were created that replaced celluloid in many items
「多くの品物でセルロイドに取って代わるような不燃性のプラスチック類が創りだされた」。
※ that以下の関係代名詞節の先行詞はplasticsで、この文は関係代名詞の先行詞が離れている例。
☐ make film　「フィルムを作る」
☐ That's why …　「そういうわけで…だ」
☐ refer to celluloid when they talk about the movies
「映画の話をするときにセルロイドに言及する」

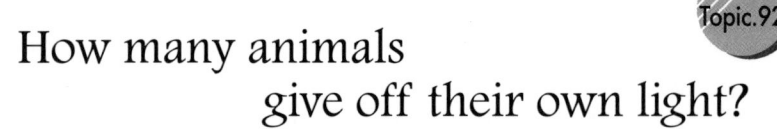

Topic.92
How many animals give off their own light?

There are 19 types of bioluminescent animals, and most of them are sea creatures. They range from bacteria and single-celled algae to fish, sharks, and squid, plus several types of insects, including the firefly. There aren't any amphibians, birds, reptiles, or mammals that are bioluminescent. Animals create light for many reasons. Some communicate with each other through it, while others use it to find food. It's like having a built-in night light!

専門用語
- bioluminescent　生物発光のalgae（algaの複数形）藻
- squid　イカ　　amphibian　両生類の動物

squid

注
- give off ～　「～（臭いや光など）を放つ、発する」
- range from A to B　「その範囲はAからBまでに及ぶ」
- plus ～　（前）「～を加えて」
- Some communicate with each other through it, while others use it to find food.
  「光を通してお互いのコミュニケーションを図っているものもいれば、その一方で食物をみつけるのにそれを使っているものもいる」
- built-in night light　「作りつけの常夜灯」

Topic.93
Why does the moon shine?

The moon doesn't produce any light – it only looks bright because it reflects light from the Sun. The moon acts like a mirror, shining sunlight back towards the Earth. Half of the moon is always lit up by the sun, but we only see parts of it because of the Earth's position in relation to the moon. This causes the phases of the moon.

[専門用語]
□ phases of the moon　（月の）相

[注]
□ reflects light from the Sun　「太陽からやってくる光を反射する」
□ the Earth's position in relation to the moon　「月に対する地球の位置」
※ in relation to 〜　「〜に関係して」

What did Jonas Salk invent?

Topic.94

Dr. Jonas Salk was a doctor and researcher who made one of the most important medical discoveries of the 20th century. In 1955, the polio vaccine that Salk created was found to be successful and was made publicly available. Before that time, the disease of polio had infected and killed millions of people around the world. Salk made the very first vaccine to prevent children from getting the disease. His vaccine and later versions have been so successful that half the planet is officially free of polio today.

[専門用語]
□ polio vaccine　ポリオワクチン

[注]
□ Dr. Jonas Salk　「ジョナス・ソーク博士」
□ and (it) was made publicly available
　「そして公に利用可能となった」
□ the very first vaccine to prevent children from getting the disease
　「子供がその病気にかかるのを防ぐまさに最初のワクチン」
cf. prevent 〜 from …ing　「〜が…するのを妨げる」
□ His vaccine and later versions
　「彼のワクチンとその後にできた改良型のワクチン」
□ half the planet　「地球の半分の地域」
□ be free of 〜　「〜を免れて」

What did Jonas Salk invent?　　　　　　　　Topic 94

参考HP　http://www.achievement.org/autodoc/page/sal0bio-1

http://hotwired.goo.ne.jp/news/technology/story/20040517306.html

What was the largest tornado ever?

Topic.95

Tornadoes are the most violent storms on Earth! According to the Storm Prediction Center, the biggest tornado ever recorded was over the high plains of Texas near the town of Gruver on June 9, 1971. It was over two miles wide at times! It's possible that larger tornadoes have existed, but nobody measured and wrote them down. The biggest outbreak of tornadoes that's been recorded was when 147 tornadoes touched down in 13 U.S. states on April 3rd and 4th in 1974.

専門用語
- [ ] tornado　トルネード(大竜巻)

注
- [ ] Storm Prediction Center　「嵐予報センター」
- [ ] the biggest tornado ever recorded
  「今までに記録されている最も大きなトルネード」
- [ ] over the high plains of Texas　「テキサスの高原を覆って」
- [ ] at times　「ときどき」
- [ ] It's possible that larger tornadoes have existed
  「それよりもっと大きなトルネードが存在した可能性はある」
- [ ] write down 〜　「〜を書きとめる、記録する」

- [ ] The biggest outbreak of tornadoes
「複数のトルネードの発生のうちで最も大きなもの」。この文の前までは、単体のトルネードの発生について言及したもの。この文以降は、複数のトルネードの同時発生について述べている。
- [ ] touch down 「上陸する」

> 参考
> Gruver はテキサス州 Hansford 郡の都市。2000年の人口調査現在は、人口1,162人であった。

How many different types of triangles are there?

Topic.96

A triangle is any three-sided polygon. All of the angles in a triangle add up to 180 degrees. There are six main types of triangles: equilateral (all sides have equal length), isosceles (two sides have equal length), scalene (all three sides have different lengths), acute (every angle is acute, or less than 90 degrees), obtuse (one angle is greater than 90 degrees), and right (one angle is exactly 90 degrees).

専門用語
- [ ] polygon 多角形   □ equilateral 等辺の
- [ ] isoscele 二等辺の □ scalene 不等辺の
- [ ] acute 鋭角の   □ obtuse 鈍角の
- [ ] right 直角の

注
- [ ] add up to ～ 「合計～になる」

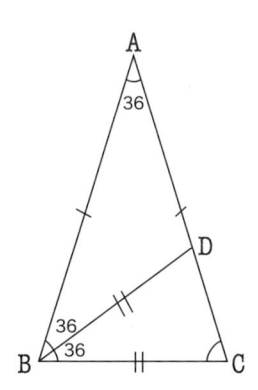

Topic.97
How come water has no taste or color?

The Dictionary defines water as "a clear, colorless, odorless, and tasteless liquid, H_2O, essential for most plant and animal life." The Encyclopedia goes on to say that "Life depends on water for virtually every process, its ability to dissolve many other substances being perhaps its most essential quality". The reason why water has no color is because light passes through it relatively easy, like a window (although large bodies of water will start to take on color since the light has to travel farther and acts differently). The reason it has no taste is because water is a very simple molecule that is a basic building block of life — we're over 80% water!

専門用語
- odorless　無臭の

注
- How come S V…?　「なぜ…なの?」
※ 疑問詞 Why と異なり、S V という語順が続く。
- go on to …　「さらに…する」
- depends on 〜 for …　「…の点で〜に頼る」
- virtually every 〜　「ほとんどすべての〜」。は、「事実上」という意味の副詞だが、almost とほぼ同じ意味でも使われる。
- its ability to dissolve many other substances being perhaps its most essential quality
  ＝ and its ability to dissolve many other substances is perhaps its most essential quality
  「他の多くの物質を溶かす能力は水の最も重要な性質であろう」。分詞構文である点に注意したい。
- light passes through it relatively easy
  「光は比較的容易に水を通過する」
※ easy はここでは副詞。
- take on color　「色を帯びる」
- water is a very simple molecule　「水はとてもシンプルな分子である」
- basic building block of life　「生命の基本的な成分(構成要素)」

Topic.98

How do broken bones heal?

Bones are living things, just like your skin or internal organs. If you break a bone, millions of tiny cells will grow and multiply to repair the break. Blood clots will close the space between the broken bones, and then your body will deposit more hard bone material to repair the damage. It's important that your bone remains very still, which is why people wear casts.

[専門用語]
□ internal organ　内臓　　□ blood clot　血の塊　　□ cast　ギプス

[注]
□ multiply　「増殖する」
□ repair the break　「破損箇所を修復する」
□ deposit more hard bone material　「さらに強固な骨の材料を蓄積する」
□ remain still　「動かない」
cf. remain ＋ 形容詞　「…のままでいる」。stillはここでは形容詞で、「静かな、静止した」

Topic.99

Why do people yawn?

The Yahooligans! Online Dictionary defines a yawn as "To open the mouth wide with a deep inhalation, usually involuntarily from drowsiness, fatigue, or boredom." As to why we yawn, all of the experts in our *Ask an Expert* category seem to agree – no one is really sure. Many scientists think that it is the body's way of taking in a quick burst of oxygen, as kind of a wake-up call. Have you ever noticed how yawns are contagious? That's another one of life's little mysteries.

[専門用語]
□ The Yahooligans! Online Dictionary
　　Yahoo!のカテゴリーの中にあるオンライン辞書
□ inhalation　息を吸いこむこと　　□ contagious　伝染性の

Why do people yawn? Topic.99

> 注

- [ ] involuntarily 「思わず知らず」
- [ ] As to why we yawn 「人がなぜあくびをするのかに関して(は)」
※ as to ～ 「～に関して」。「前置詞＋名詞節」の形。
- [ ] all of the experts in our *Ask an Expert* category
「Yahoo!の*Ask an Expert*というカテゴリーの中の専門家はすべて」
- [ ] take in a quick burst of oxygen 「酸素をすばやく一気に吸収する」
cf. take in ～ 「～を吸収する」。burst「突発、激発、噴出、一気」
(例) a burst of laughter [applause] どっと起る笑い[拍手]
- [ ] kind of ～ 「どちらかというと～」
- [ ] wake-up call 「注意喚起、(ホテルなどの)モーニングコール」
- [ ] That's another ～ 「それもまた～だ」
- [ ] life's little mysteries 「人生のちょっとしたミステリー」

How high can birds fly?

Topic.100

According to Guinness World Records, a Ruppell's vulture flew at 37,000 feet, where it collided with a plane over the Côte d'Ivoire in 1973. That's the highest recorded bird flight ever. Bar-headed geese are probably the birds that fly highest on a regular basis. They breed in Tibet and winter in India, so they have to fly over 18,000 feet to get through the Himalayan Mountains. Bar-headed geese have been seen flying at 28,000 feet high. Demoiselle cranes, godwits, and curlew have also been seen flying around Mount Everest at 20,000 feet. The Himalayan snow cock nests at those high altitudes too. Those are some high-flying birds!

> 専門用語

- [ ] Ruppell's vulture マダラハゲワシ
- [ ] the Côte d'Ivoire コートジボワール共和国(西アフリカの国。かつては日本語に訳して象牙海岸と呼んでいた)
- [ ] Demoiselle crane アネハヅル   □ godwit オグロシギ
- [ ] curlew シャクシギ   □ Himalayan snow cock ヒマラヤセッケイ

注

- on a regular basis 「定期的に」
- Bar-headed goose 「インドガン」。(geese は goose の複数形)
- get through the Himalayan Mountains 「ヒマラヤ山脈を越える」
- breed in Tibet 「チベットで子を産む」
- and (they) winter in India 「インドで冬を過ごす」
- ※ このwinterは動詞で、冬を過ごす、越冬する」という意味。
- have been seen flying 「飛んでいるところを目撃された」
- around Mount Everest 「エベレスト山の周りを」
- nests at those high altitudes 「そのような高い標高のところに巣を作る」
- high-flying bird 「高いところを飛ぶ鳥」

Topic. 101

What are amoebas?

Amoebas are microbes – that means they are living organisms too small to be seen with the naked eye. You can only see them through a microscope. They're a very simple kind of animal that lives in water or where it's damp. While you and I have trillions of cells in our body, amoebas are made of just one cell! Their shape changes constantly as they move, and they have false feet called pseudopodia that they use to swim and to capture and eat tiny animals and plants. Amoebas reproduce by splitting in half in a process called fission.

専門用語

- amoeba アメーバ microbe 微生物
- pseudopodia 仮足(細胞質の一時的な突起)
- reproduce 繁殖する fission 分裂

amoeba

What are amoebas? 　　Topic. 101

[注]

☐ living organisms too small to be seen with the naked eye
「小さすぎて裸眼では見えない生物」
※ too small …以下は形容詞句で、直前のliving organismsを修飾している。
cf. too ～ to …　「～すぎて…できない」
☐ trillions of cells　「何兆個もの細胞」
☐ amoebas are made of just one cell
「アメーバはたった一つの細胞でできている」
☐ false feet　「ニセの足」
☐ split in half　「半分に裂ける」

Are chimpanzees the smartest monkeys in the world?　　Topic. 102

Chimpanzees are very smart, but they're not monkeys. Over 233 species of primates are classified into three groups – monkeys, apes (which includes chimpanzees), and prosimians. So chimps are related to monkeys. But did you know that chimps are more closely related to us than to any other animal? Chimpanzees and humans share 98.4% of the same DNA. Maybe that's why chimps are so smart! The Lincoln Park Zoo says that chimpanzees are better at problem solving than any animal other than humans. Researchers have even taught chimps to talk with American Sign Language. The Chimpanzee and Human Communication Institute observes four chimps who talk in sign language, and the mother chimp even taught sign language to her son!

[専門用語]

☐ primate　霊長類の動物　　☐ prosimian　原猿

[注]

☐ are classified into three groups
「3つのグループに分類することができる」

- ☐ monkeys, apes (which includes chimpanzees), and prosimians
  「サル、類人猿(チンパンジーはこれに含まれる)、原猿(キツネザル、アイアイが属する)」
- ☐ chimps are related to monkeys 「チンパンジーはサルと関係している」
- cf. chimpはchimpanzeeの簡略形
- ※ be related to ～ 「～と関係がある」
- ☐ are more closely related to us than to any other animal
  「チンパンジーは他の動物よりも人とより密接な関係がある」
- ☐ share 98.4% of the same DNA
  「同じDNAを98.4%共有する」≒「チンパンジーと人のDNAの違いは1.6%だけだ」
- ☐ are better at problem solving 「問題解決が、より得意だ」
- ※ be good at ～ (～が得意だ)の比較級
- ☐ other than ～ 「～以外に、～以外の」
- ☐ teach chimps to talk 「チンパンジーが話をすることができるように教える」
- ☐ American Sign Language 「アメリカサインランゲージ」。アメリカ手話言語。アメリカ・カナダなどで大半の聾者が母語として用いている自然言語の手話。直前のwithは、「～を使って」。

How many countries speak Spanish?

Topic. 103

The World Factbook has detailed profiles of every country in the world. So I looked through the population pages for each country and found out what languages are most commonly spoken there. These countries speak Spanish as their first, only, or official language: Argentina, Bolivia, Chile, Columbia, Costa Rica, Cuba, Dominican Republic, Ecuador, El Salvador, Equatorial Guinea, Guatemala, Honduras, Mexico, Nicaragua, Panama, Paraguay, Peru, Puerto Rico, Spain, Uruguay, and Venezuela. Spanish is also spoken in Aruba, Belize, Brazil, Gibraltar, Netherlands Antilles, Trinidad and Tobago, Virgin Islands, and the United States, but it's not the main language in these places. You could talk with all of Central and South America if you speak Spanish!

How many countries speak Spanish?

Topic. 103

専門用語
- World Factbook　世界の統計を集めたYahoo! 内のサイト名

注
- look through 〜　「〜を調べる、〜に目を通す」
- speak Spanish as their first, only, or official language
  「第一言語または唯一の言語あるいは公式言語としてスペイン語を話す」
- Argentina「アルゼンチン」、Bolivia「ボリビア」、Chile「チリ」、Columbia「コロンビア」、Costa Rica「コスタリカ」、Cuba「キューバ」、Dominican Republic「ドミニカ共和国」、Ecuador「エクアドル」、El Salvador「エルサルバドル」、Equatorial Guinea「赤道ギニア」、Guatemala「グアテマラ」、Honduras「ホンジュラス」、Mexico「メキシコ」、Nicaragua「ニカラグア」、Panama「パナマ」、Paraguay「パラグアイ」、Peru「ペルー」、Puerto Rico「プエルトリコ」、Spain「スペイン」、Uruguay「ウルグアイ」、and Venezuela「ベネズエラ」
- Aruba「アルーバ(中南米)」、Belize「ベリーズ(中米)」、Brazil「ブラジル」、Gibraltar「ジブラルタル(スペイン南端近くの狭い半島にある要塞化された港市)」、Netherlands Antilles「オランダ領アンティル諸島(カリブ海にある数島からなるオランダの自治領)」、Trinidad and Tobago「トリニダード・トバゴ共和国（西インド諸島の中の独立国。英連邦の一員」、Virgin Islands「バージン諸島(西インド諸島北東部。米領と英領に分かれている)」、and the United States「アメリカ合衆国」
- You could talk with all of Central and South America if you speak Spanish!
  「もしもあなたがスペイン語を話すことができれば、中南米のすべての諸国と話ができるかもしれない」。厳密にいうと、「諸国の人々と話す」だが、ここでは国を擬人化している。またこの文ではif節の中を仮定法にしないで、帰結節だけを仮定法にしている。これはif節の内容を現実味のあるものにして、帰結節の内容は少し控えめに表現したもの。(スペイン語をしゃべることができるようになるのは努力次第で可能。それを実際に使って現地の人々と話をすることができるかどうかは、その時の事情次第であるが…というニュアンス)

Topic. 104

How does yeast grow?

Yeast is actually a tiny, one-celled fungus that grows by dividing into two pieces. Each piece becomes a whole yeast cell itself, and they keep splitting and growing new cells. Just like plants and animals, yeast needs water, food, and warmth to grow. Yeast's favorite foods are sugar, the fructose and glucose found in fruit and honey, and maltose from flour. Yeast eats this food and produces carbon dioxide and alcohol – that's why people use yeast to make bread and alcoholic drinks. In bread, the carbon dioxide bubbles are caught in the dough and create a light, airy texture. Take a close look at a slice of bread, and you'll see the bubbles.

|専門用語|

- ☐ yeast　イースト(酵母菌)　☐ fungus　菌類
- ☐ fructose　果糖　☐ glucose　ぶどう糖　☐ maltose　麦芽糖
- ☐ dough　パン生地

|注|

- ☐ sugar, the fructose and glucose found in fruit and honey, and maltose from flour
  「糖類すなわち、果物や蜂蜜の中にある果糖やぶどう糖、そして小麦粉から取れる麦芽糖」
- ☐ produces carbon dioxide and alcohol
  「炭酸ガスとアルコールを生成する」。(その過程は発酵である)
- ☐ carbon dioxide bubbles
  「二酸化炭素の気泡」。要するに、イーストが生成する二酸化炭素は、パンをふっくらとさせるのに役立っているということ。
- ☐ light, airy texture　「軽くてふんわりとしたきめ」
- cf. texture　「組織、外見、きめ」
- ☐ Take a close look at ～　「～をよく見てごらんなさい」

参考HP: http://www.nitten.co.jp/question/question10.htm

Who invented the cassette tape?

Topic. 105

It's hard to credit just one inventor with the cassette tape because there were different versions over the years. Magnetic recording is how cassettes capture sound. A Danish engineer, Valdemar Poulsen, patented a magnetized recording device in 1898. Poulsen's machine recorded on wire, but later inventors like Fritz Pfleumer used strips of plastic to record magnetically. An American inventor, Marvin Camras, made important improvements to magnetic tape recording during World War II. Finally, in 1963, the Philips Company introduced the compact cassette tape, which is a lot like the ones we still use.

|専門用語|
- ☐ Valdemar Poulsen
  ワルデマール・ポウルセン（当時デンマークのコペンハーゲン電話会社の技師であった）
- ☐ Fritz Pfleumer　フリッツ・フロイマー（ドイツの技術者）

|注|
- ☐ credit A with B　「AにBの功績があると思う」
  ≒ credit B to A
  （参考）古い辞書には掲載されていないが、最新の語法では認められている。
- ☐ magnetic recording　「磁気録音、磁気記録」
- ☐ how cassettes capture sound　「カセットが音をとらえる方法」
- ☐ patented a magnetized recording device in 1898
  「1898年に磁気記録装置の特許を取得した」
- ☐ recorded on wire
  「線の上に記録した」。ポウルセンはピアノ線を使用した。
- ☐ used strips of plastic to record magnetically
  「磁気を利用して記録するのにプラスチックの細長いきれを使った」。フリッツはドイツでプラスチックテープ地に鉄粉を塗った磁気テープを発明した。(1928年)
- ☐ compact cassette tape　「コンパクト・カセット・テープ」

参考HP http://contest.thinkquest.gr.jp/tqj1998/10157/word/txt9071.htm

How are oceans formed?

Topic. 106

Did you know that millions of years ago, Earth had no oceans? At one time the Earth's surface was so hot that water boiled away. But volcanoes spewed steam into the atmosphere, and eventually the Earth cooled down. The water droplets in the steam condensed and fell as rain. For thousands of years, rain poured down on the planet to create the first oceans. Today, 71% of the planet's surface is covered by water! All of the Earth's oceans are interconnected, and the same water circulates through them. The water cycle keeps the oceans full. Water from the ocean evaporates and rises into the clouds. The clouds create rain and snow, which fall to the ground and fill the oceans (and lakes too).

専門用語

☐ spew　吐き出す　☐ droplet　小滴
☐ interconnect　相互に連絡する

注

☐ boil away　「(液体が沸騰して)蒸発する」
☐ condensed and fell as rain　「凝結して雨として落ちた」
☐ rain poured down on the planet to create the first oceans
　「雨が地球に激しく降り、(その結果)最初の海ができた」
☐ water cycle　「水の循環」。The water cycle keeps the oceans full.
　→水は地球規模で循環しているので、たとえばどこかの大洋だけに水がないという事態は起こらない。

What is soil made of?

Topic. 107

The outermost layer of our Earth is soil, and that's formed from eroding rocks and decaying plants and animals. Fungi and bacteria break down organic matter to turn it into soil, and plant roots help break up rocks to become soil. Animals like mice help make soil too – the burrows they dig help mix up the soil. Earthworms make the soil richer by digesting organic matter and recycling nutrients. All these natural processes can take over 500 years to create just one inch of topsoil! On average, soil is made of 45 percent minerals, 25 percent water, 25 percent air, and five percent organic matter. Who knew dirt was this complicated?

専門用語

- ☐ outermost　最も外側の　☐ erode　浸食される、浸食する
- ☐ fungi　fungus（菌類）の複数形
- ☐ burrow　（小動物が掘った）穴
- ☐ topsoil　表土　☐ dirt　土

注

- ☐ outermost layer of our Earth　「地球の最も外側の（地）層」
- ☐ eroding rocks and decaying plants and animals
  「浸食された岩や朽ちた動植物」
- ☐ break down organic matter　「有機物を分解する」
- ☐ plant roots help (to) break up rocks to become soil
  「植物の根は岩を壊して、それが土になる手助けをしている」
- cf. break up ～　「～を壊す、細分化する」
- ※ help (to) …　「…するのを助ける、…するのに役立つ」
- ☐ the burrows they dig help (to) mix up the soil
  「そのような動物が掘った穴は土が混ざり合うのに役立つ」
- cf. mix up ～　「～をよく混ぜ合わす」。→その穴の空間に、やがて四方から土が流れ込むことによって土同士が混ざり合うということ。
- ☐ earthworm　「ミミズ」

注

☐ and (by) recycling nutrients
「そして栄養物を再循環させることによって」

> (参考)ミミズは土の中の有機物を摂取して分解しているが、そのフンは栄養に富んでいて、それが土を肥沃なものにするという仕組みである。

☐ All these natural processes can take over 500 years to create just one inch of topsoil!
「以上のような自然のプロセスは、たった1インチの表土を創るのに500年以上もかかることだってありうる」

cf. take over（〜を引き継ぐ）と読み間違えないように。「時間がかかる」という意味のtakeと、「〜以上」という意味のoverである。over 500 years「500年以上」。新たに土ができるまでには膨大な時間がかかるということだ。

☐ on average 「平均して」
☐ Who knew dirt was this complicated?
「土がこんなに複雑なものだったなんて、いったい誰が知っていただろうか」
※ 反語的表現。thisはここでは副詞で、「こんなに、これほどまでに」

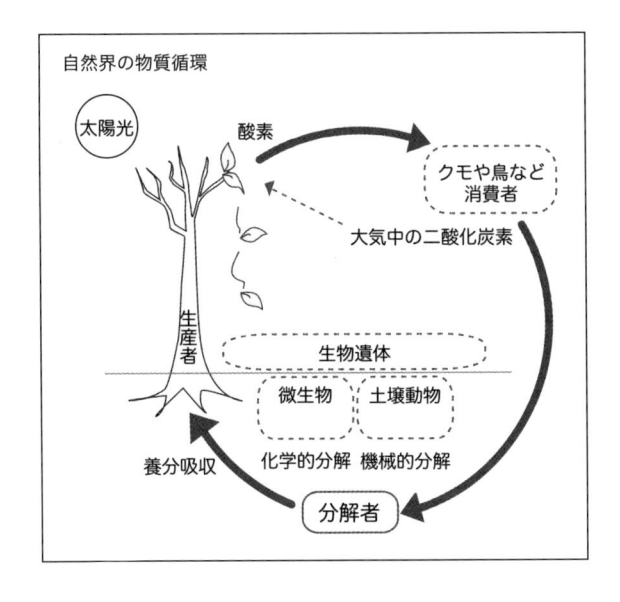

自然界の物質循環

太陽光 / 酸素 / クモや鳥など消費者 / 大気中の二酸化炭素 / 生産者 / 生物遺体 / 微生物 / 土壌動物 / 養分吸収 / 化学的分解 機械的分解 / 分解者

Who invented popcorn?

Topic. 108

Folks have been popping corn for thousands of years. In fact, archeologists discovered some very stale popcorn in New Mexico that was about 4,000 years old! Even with extra butter that would still be pretty chewy. Popcorn was very important to the Aztecs, who not only ate it but used it as decoration in their religious ceremonies. And during World War II, when sugar was rationed in the U.S., popcorn became a popular substitute for candy.

専門用語
- New Mexico （アメリカの）ニューメキシコ州
- chewy 噛み応えのある
- Aztec アステカ族の人(メキシコ中部に文明を築いていたアメリカインディアンの一部族) □ ration （供給を）制限する

注
- Folks 「人々」
- butter that would still be pretty chewy
  「もしも実際に噛んでみたら噛み応えがするであろうバター」
  ※ この助動詞wouldは仮定法を作るために用いられている。
- popular substitute for candy
  「キャンディーの代用品として人気のあるもの」。砂糖の供給が制限されたため十分な量のキャンディーが作れなくなった。そのため間食用にポップコーンが人気のあるものになった。

How do magnets work?

Topic. 109

Magnetism is a force that makes objects attract or repel one another. A magnet starts with a piece of metal that can be magnetized, such as iron, steel, or nickel. Inside these metals are molecules called magnetic domains that have both a north and south pole of magnetic force. In unmagnetized metals, the poles point every which way. But the ones inside a magnet point in the same direction, and this gives the whole magnet a north pole and a south pole, creating a magnetic field. If you put the north end of one magnet near the south end of another magnet, they'll pull towards each other. But if you put a north end near a north or a south end near a south, they'll push away from each other.

[専門用語]
- □ magnetism　磁力　□ every which way　四方八方に、ふぞろいに
- □ unmagnetized metals　磁化されていない金属

[注]
- □ makes objects attract or repel one another
「お互いを引っ張ったりはね返したりする」
- □ magnetize ～　「～を磁化する」。「磁化」は専門用語だが、たとえば鉄、ニッケル、コバルトなどの磁性を持ちうる物質に強力な磁石を近づけると、やがてはそれ自身も磁石になる。この過程を、「磁化」という。
- □ Inside these metals are molecules called magnetic domains
「これらの金属の内部には磁区と呼ばれる分子が存在している」
※ 主語(molecules)と述語動詞(are)が倒置した文。
these metalsとは前文の iron, steel, or nickel(鉄、鋼、ニッケルなど)をさし、もっと厳密にいうとmetal that can be magnetized(磁化されうる金属)のこと。これらの金属は、「強磁性元素」ということもできる。

(参考)ただし現在では、科学技術が飛躍的に進歩し、以上のような単体の強磁性元素を磁石として使っているだけではない。たとえば、磁気テープの磁性粉としては、マグネタイト(Fe_3O_4)などが使われているし、さらに、「フェライト磁石」といって、鉄酸化物の粉末に、バリウムやストロンチウムの微量添加物を加えて混合してできる磁石が非常に多くの最先端分野で活躍している。
なお、磁石はいくら小さな単位に切っても、小さな磁石ができるばかりで、N極のみ、S極のみを単独で取り出せない。つまり、磁石は非常に小さな磁石が集まってできていると考えられている。内部ではそれら(つまり小さな磁石)の向きがほとんど揃っていて、その集合体が磁石として働いている。そのような小さな磁石を専門用語では「スピン」と呼んでいる。そのスピンが同じ方向を向いた領域のことを「磁区」といっている。

Topic. 109

How do magnets work?
- □ a north and south pole of magnetic force 「磁力のN極とS極」
- □ magnetic field 「磁場、磁界」

参考HP　岡山大学
http://www.magnet.okayama-u.ac.jp/magword/domain/

(参考：TDK) 電磁誘導の発見に苦闘したファラデー
(http://www.tdk.co.jp/techmag/ninja/daa31000.htm)
自転車の発電ランプは、電球が切れる以外、故障もほとんどなく、そのため分解しにくいつくりになっています。それをあえてコジアケると、図のような構造になっていることが分かります。自転車のタイヤが回ると、トックリ状の発電機上部の回転軸が回転し、内部の円筒形の磁石を回します。磁石の下、すなわちトックリの底にはコイルが置かれているので、このコイルから電流を取り出していることも想像できます。しかし、円筒形の磁石が回転することで、なぜコイルに電流が発生するのでしょうか？
　ここで発電機の歴史を振り返ってみることにしましょう。1820年にエルステッドは、針金に電流を流すと、そばに置かれた方位磁石の針が振れることから、電流は磁気を生み出すことを発見しました。電流が磁気をつくるのなら、逆に磁石を利用して電流をつくりだせるはずだと考えたのはファラデーです。約10年 にも及ぶ試行錯誤ののち、ファラデーは1831年、磁石を動かして磁場を変化させたときにコイルに電流が流れるという有名な「電磁誘導の法則」を発見し、その翌年には初歩的な発電機も考案しました。しかし、これは実用には不向きで、同年にピクシーが発明した手回し式の発電機が世界最初の発電機といわれています。U字型の磁石とコイルを巻いた鉄心を向かい合わせに置き、ハンドルで磁石を回転させて磁場を変化させると、コイルに交流電流が発生します。
(参考：TDK：しかし、磁石の磁性のルーツは、強磁性元素(鉄、コバルト、ニッケル、希土類元素の一部)のもつ磁性電子にあるのですから、合金でも金属酸化物でもかまわなかったのです。また、強磁性元素に他の元素が加わることで強い磁性が発現するのが磁石の不思議なところで、単独の強磁性元素だけではすぐれた磁石にはなりません。)

磁気テープの磁性粉は酸化鉄のミニ磁石
(http://www.tdk.co.jp/techmag/daa00213.htm)
磁気テープの磁性粉としては、マグネタイト(Fe_3O_4)やマグヘマイト(γ-Fe_2O_3)の結晶粒子を針状に成長させたものが使用されます。
未使用テープに塗布された磁性粉はまだ磁化されていない微細な棒磁石です。ここに磁気ヘッドの磁界が加わると、磁石としての性質に目覚めて磁化されます。磁性粉は半磁石として磁化を保持するので、記録された情報は何度でも再生できます。しかし、磁性粉は永久磁石ほどガンコな性質をもたないので、新たな磁界が加えられたときは、容易に磁化の向きを変えます。使用したテープを再利用できる のもこのためです。
こうした磁化過程をグラフで表すと、独特のS字ループを描くヒステリシスカーブ（磁気履歴曲線）となります。磁気ヘッドの磁界が加わると、磁性粉は磁化されて磁気飽和状態にまで達します。しかし、いったん磁石としての性質に目覚めたあとは、逆向きの磁界を加えても未磁化状態（グラフの原点）には戻らないので、S 字ループを描くことになります。
エレクトロニクスの黎明期であった19世紀末に、初めて登場した磁気録音というのは、当時の第一線の科学者・技術者にも、まるで忍法を見るかのような不思議な物理現象でした。それから１世紀を経て、テープレコーダが珍しい存在でなくなった今日では、この不思議さ・面白さがあまり顧みられなくなりました。これは料理でいうなら、最もおいしい部分を食べ残しているようなもので、実にもったいない話なのかもしれません。

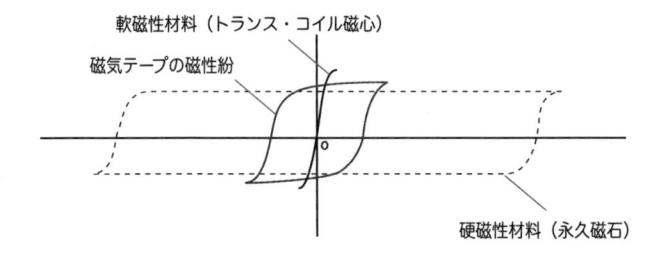

図：強磁性体のタイプとヒステリシスカーブ

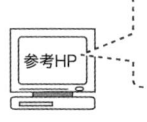

参考HP　TDK 月刊「テクマグ」じしゃく忍法帳 第３回と29回
http://www.tdk.co.jp/techmag/ninja/index.htm

How do cats land on their four legs when they fall?

Topic. 110

While cats are very agile, or quick with their body, they don't always land on their feet when they fall. If they leap after a bird and fall more than twenty feet, they will probably hurt themselves. But in a shorter fall, a cat quickly figures out which way is up and turns its head right side up. Then it twists the upper body around to land with its front paws on the ground. The hind paws naturally follow behind. Cats can do this because they have a very sensitive vestibular apparatus, which is a fluid-filled organ in the inner ear that helps them determine which way is up. In the Middle Ages, people thought that cats were evil. They prowled around at night, and their eyes glowed creepily, so they must have been sent by the devil!

専門用語

- [ ] the vestibular apparatus (of the ear)　内耳前庭器官
- [ ] prowl around　徘徊する　　□ creepily　気味悪く

注

- [ ] on their four legs　「４本の足が地に着いて」

※正しい着地を表現している。接触の意味を表す前置詞onが使われている。
- [ ] While cats are very agile, or quick with their body
  「ネコは自分の身体に関しては機敏で迅速な行動を取る動物なのだが」
- [ ] they don't always land on their feet
  「かならずしも足で着地するとはかぎらない」

cf. not always … 「かならずしも…とはかぎらない」。部分否定である。
- [ ] leap after a bird and fall more than twenty feet
  「鳥を追って跳躍し、２０フィート以上も落ちる」

※　前置詞afterが、「〜を追跡して」という意味で使われている。この文では高い木の枝などから落ちる場合を想定しているのであろう。
- [ ] in a shorter fall　「落下距離が短い場合には」。たとえば、人間の目の高さくらいなところで実験してみるとよい。ネコを仰向けの状態にしてそのまま手を放す。ネコは上手に回転して必ずうまく着地するのである。
- [ ] figure out 〜　「〜を理解する」＝ make out 〜

- □ right side up　「表を上にして」。ここは「its head、つまりネコの頭の正しい側を上に向けて」という意味。反対はwrong side up「逆さに、逆さまに」（間違った側を上にして）。仮に転倒するような場合を考えてみると、たとえば鼻の部分が空を向いた状態になるだろう。その場合、wrong side（あるべきではない側）が上に向くことになる。
- □ twists the upper body around to land　「上半身をひねって着地する」
- □ with its front paws on the ground　「前足を地につけて」

※ 前置詞withを使って付帯状況を表している。

cf. with ～(its front paws) …(on the ground)　「～を…の状態にして」
- □ a fluid-filled organ in the inner ear　「内耳にある流動体で満たされた器官」
- □ must have been sent　「送られたにちがいない」

cf. must have＋過去分詞で、「…したにちがいない」

At what temperature does water boil?

Topic. 111

It all depends on your altitude! Different levels of atmospheric pressure make water boil at different temperatures. This is because at higher altitudes, there is less pressure keeping the water in a liquid state, so it can boil at a lower temperature. For example, you can boil water on top of Mount Everest much quicker than at sea level. The standard boiling point at sea level, however, is around one hundred degrees Celsius.

注

- □ Different levels of atmospheric pressure make water boil at different temperatures.
  「大気圧の大きさが異なれば、水が沸騰する温度も異なる」
- □ pressure keeping the water in a liquid state
  「水を液体の状態に維持する気圧」
- □ at sea level　「海面で」。つまり、「海抜０メートルで」
- □ around one hundred degrees Celsius　「およそ摂氏100度」

参考

水の沸点は、富士山頂上で約80度、エベレスト頂上では70度くらいだと言われている。低い温度で沸騰するということは、水がこれ以上の温度にならないということなのだから、おいしい料理は期待できないという結果になるね。

本書には
カセットテープ
(別売)が
あります。

Gateway to Science
from Yahoo! Ask Earl
―子供の素直な不思議に答える111のキー―

2006年1月20日　初版発行
2022年3月31日　重版発行
編著者　風早 寛
発行者　福岡正人
発行所　株式会社 金星堂
〒101-0051 東京都千代田区神田神保町3-21
Tel　(03)3263-3828
Fax　(03)3263-0716
http://www.kinsei-do.co.jp
e-mail: text@kinsei-do.co.jp

編集担当　佐川弘明
印刷所　興亜産業(株)
1-23-3825
落丁・乱丁本はお取り替えいたします。
ISBN978-4-7647-3825-6　　C1082